I am delighted with Myles Munroe's newest book, *The Burden of Freedom*. Perhaps better than anyone I know who is influential worldwide, Myles is better able to describe the burden of freedom, particularly in Third World nations, and give an answer from God THAT REALLY WORKS.

A fascinating book by one of our finest writers.

—ORAL ROBERTS
FOUNDER/CHANCELLOR
ORAL ROBERTS UNIVERSITY

My dear friend of over twenty-five years, Dr. Myles Munroe, is one of the most profound thinkers of our day. He is largely responsible for awakening the idea of "purpose" in the hearts and minds of countless thousands (perhaps millions) around the world. I have no doubt that through Dr. Myles's latest revelation, *The Burden of Freedom*, countless more will be awakened to the idea of freedom, not only as an ethereal, spiritual concept, but more so that they will become aware of their own freedom and begin to possess the land of promise and prosperity that was originally intended for them and for which they were born.

—BISHOP CARLTON D. PEARSON
PRESIDING BISHOP, AZUSA INTERDENOMINATIONAL FELLOWSHIP
SENIOR PASTOR, HIGHER DIMENSIONS FAMILY CHURCH
TULSA, OKLAHOMA

Dr. Myles Munroe so adequately presents to the reader in his book *The Burden of Freedom* that freedom is not the absence of law, work or a release from authority, but in reality, true freedom imposes more law and more work than slavery, because it demands more discipline and self-control than slavery.

He shows us that true management is the management of our selves and our environment and that it is the ultimate purpose of God for mankind as he shows us that freedom is the responsibility of a return to stewardship.

He challenges the reader to dominate an area of earth with his or her gift and an open heart, and thereby experience the freedom awaiting in the land of promise—the land of milk and honey.

—DR. FUCHSIA T. PICKETT
AUTHOR AND SPEAKER

This is another challenging book by renowned author Dr. Myles Munroe, which is a must-read for all those who want to understand what true freedom is. Most people think that freedom means a license to do whatever they please, without any restriction, limitation, accountability or responsibility. Dr. Munroe tells us in this book that freedom comes with a price tag and reminds us that freedom should not be used as an opportunity to do wrong. (See Galatians 5:1.) Dr. Munroe ably answers questions such as why freedom is so difficult to achieve and why we become prisoners of our own inventions and victims of our modern products.

I highly recommend this book to those who want to be truly free and who want to use their freedom to bring this under-standing and hope to others who do not have this knowledge and are still under the yoke of slavery in all its different guises.

—DR. KENNETH MESHOE, MP
MEMBER OF PARLIAMENT
PRESIDENT OF AFRICAN CHRISTIAN DEMOCRATIC PARTY
SOUTH AFRICAN GOVERNMENT

Have you been confused at times by the competing claims of communism and capitalism as the key to freedom?

Have you ever had occasion to marvel how, in describing certain events done in certain places allegedly in pursuit of freedom, the words *ethnic cleansing* are used and when, in describing similar events in some other places, the words *tribal warfare* are used?

Perhaps it was because we did not have a clear under-standing of what freedom entailed and what it meant. Perhaps we just lost sight of the fact that freedom requires humanity and tolerance.

Whatever the case may be, this book by Dr. Myles Munroe reminds us that freedom is not a freebie—that it has a price, that it requires sacrifice and self-imposed discipline. Indeed, it makes it clear that freedom is not a license to live and do as we please, but that it has inherent responsibilities.

I thank and congratulate Dr. Munroe for his insightful analysis of the burdens of freedom, and I commend it to persons of goodwill everywhere.

—SIR LYNDEN PINDLING
FORMER PRIME MINISTER OF THE COMMONWEALTH OF THE BAHAMAS

Dr. Myles Munroe is a multitalented individual with extraordinary insight into the development of human potential, and he promotes relationships of trust and respect. Through example he continues to inspire mankind with his vision and leadership. Dr. Munroe is an outstanding spiritual leader who does not compromise his belief or core values.

This book, *The Burden of Freedom,* deals with harsh realities. It outlines the problems of democratic tyranny but yet defines God's plan for freedom. It is written at a time in history when the people of the world actively search for freedom and the opportunity to create a life that has both purpose and possibility, a life that has hope.

The fall of totalitarian governments gives each of us a moment for celebration, and momentarily the world feels safe as the threat of military confrontation and nuclear annihilation recedes. Yet we find ourselves somewhat troubled by the lack of our understanding of freedom.

While we have been quick to acknowledge the freedom of East Germany and its unification with West Germany, we seem not to recognize the effect of this freedom and the immediate reaction once the cost for freedom was realized. We do not relate this relevance to our own lives and recognize that freedom is in the mind. In a fundamental way this book is about the application of learning how to create alternative strategies for truly freeing ourselves.

In many ways we as a people are profoundly concerned about our belief. We live with political institutions that celebrate the rights of individuals to express themselves, to assemble, to pursue happiness and individual purposes, to pick their own political leaders. We pay enormous attention to the fights and procedures of due process.

At times we seem to be on the edge of anarchy, and yet in a coherent fashion we hold on to our political beliefs and rituals with all their flaws and contradictions. Yet when we enter the lobby of the business cathedrals in our cities, we leave our belief in democratic principles at home. The halls and chambers of these buildings have flourished on a very different set of beliefs and rituals.

In this world, political correctness or silence replaces freedom of speech; demands for due process become insubordination; and disagreement with those above us draws criticisms and intimidation.

As individuals, we must be capable and responsible for pursuing our own happiness and pursuit of purpose, meaning and structure. Programs on excellence, quality and values empower strategic planning and leadership skills.

This book offers a reciprocative alternative; it is not about extolling virtue of trying harder at what we have been doing. It is about revolution. Not violent revolution, but a revolution of new ways of identifying freedom that places its hope in democratic principles. It is a book that questions the governance structures and systems of our economic institutions and lends sound biblical principles to deal with every characteristic of slavery.

Nothing is as powerful as understanding how to free yourself from the bondage of self-slavery. What makes this book important is the introduction of a new concept into the marketplace of business and industry. Not only is this work an alternative to self-imposed slavery; it is, as well, unique.

—RICHARD C. DEMERITTE
FORMER HIGH COMMISSIONER, UNITED KINGDOM
FORMER AMBASSADOR EXTRAORDINARY AND PLENIPOTENTIARY
REPUBLIC OF GERMANY
REPUBLIC OF FRANCE
EUROPEAN ECONOMIC COMMUNITY
KINGDOM OF BELGIUM
FORMER AUDITOR GENERAL OF THE BAHAMAS

The Burden of Freedom

The Burden of Freedom

Myles Munroe

THE BURDEN OF FREEDOM by Myles Munroe
Published by Creation House
A part of Strang Communications Company
600 Rinehart Road
Lake Mary, Florida 32746
www.creationhouse.com

Unless otherwise noted, all Scripture quotations are from the New International Version of the Bible. Copyright © 1973, 1978, 1984, International Bible Society. Used by permission.

Scripture quotations marked KJV are from the King James Version of the Bible.

Scripture quotations marked NKJV are from the New King James Version of the Bible. Copyright © 1979, 1980, 1982 by Thomas Nelson, Inc., publishers. Used by permission.

Scripture quotations marked NAS are taken from the New American Standard Bible. Copyright © The Lockman Foundation 1960, 1962, 1963, 1968, 1971, 1972, 1973, 1975, 1977. Used by permission. (www.Lockman.org)

Library of Congress Catalog Card Number: 96-85719
International Standard Book Number: 0-88419-446-9

0 1 2 3 4 5 6 7 VERSA 8 7 6 5 4 3 2 1
Printed in the United States of America

To the resilient human spirit buried under centuries of oppression and inhumane treatment screaming for freedom to express its true potential.

To the billions of individuals categorized as Third World people who have yet to fully participate in and benefit from the vast resources and products of the industrial revolution.

To the renowned and unknown champions, both past and present, who gave their best and paid the ultimate price for the deliverance and freedom of people.

To the generation destined to go beyond deliverance into the land of true freedom to experience the fullness of God's purpose and plan for mankind.

To the Truth who sets us free, and His ultimate sacrifice, which made my freedom possible.

The journey to true freedom requires the help of many along the way. We are all products of the input, investment, encouragement, criticism, knowledge and advice of many individuals whom we are privileged to meet along the way of life. This manuscript is the culmination of the work and support of many of these special people in my life.

I would like to thank Stephen Strang and the great staff of Creation House, who believed in the potential of this project: Rick Nash for his persistent pursuit of me in spite of my hectic travel schedule; Mark Norris for his humble spirit and helpful input in the development of the manuscript; Barbara Dycus for her coming on at the last stages and making it work.

I must also thank the members and leadership team of Bahamas Faith Ministries International, on whom I had the privilege of testing and sharing the ideas in this book.

My understanding of freedom was greatly inspired by my friends and colleagues in the International Third World Leaders Association, a group of leaders committed to the freedom of all people, especially those in Third World developing nations. Thank you.

Finally, there are the people whose support and belief in me make my work possible: My darling wife, Ruth; my precious children, Charisa and Chairo (Myles, Jr.); my late mother, Louise; my beloved father, Matthias Munroe; and those throughout the world whom I am privileged to call friends. Thank you.

Contents

FOREWORD

Dr. Myles Munroe has used this treatise as a means of giving clarity to the word *freedom,* which is often misstated and misunderstood. He challenges the notion that freedom can be manifested without the assumption of responsibility and accountability. He also puts freedom in a context that bespeaks a much higher and nobler meaning than is understood by many persons who use the term so loosely.

Dr. Munroe answers poignant questions about freedom relative to the age of technology and E-commerce, which has evolved with meteoric speed. On one level, this evolution has freed society from the bondage of functioning according to historical managerial patterns. However, it has also caused many to become enslaved to a system that has the potential to stymie creativity and intellectual development. He helps us to understand that freedom comes at a price.

Freedom for Dr. Munroe is the central theme and value of Christianity, so he challenges us to seek freedom, but to do so with a desire to maintain our value systems and to exhibit wisdom and character. Ultimately, he impresses upon us the central idea that the journey from slavery to freedom is a difficult though necessary one. But as we take the journey, we must not leave behind the principles and practices that help us to live a truly free life. Implied in this is the spiritual truth that "those whom the Lord sets free are free indeed."

—THE HONORABLE REV. FLOYD H. FLAKE
PASTOR
U.S. CONGRESSMAN, RETIRED

PREFACE

IT IS A fact no one can deny—today freedom stands unchallenged as the supreme goal and value of the Western world. Scholars and philosophers have investigated and debated it endlessly; it is the catchword of every politician, the secular gospel of our economic free-enterprise system and the foundation of all our cultural activities. Freedom is the one value for which many people, by their words and actions, often seem prepared to die. During the era of the Cold War, leaders of the West divided the world into two regional camps—the free world and the unfree world—and were willing to fight a nuclear war to defend this sacred ideal.

For many years now I have traveled throughout the world as a conference speaker, seminar teacher, university lecturer, government consultant, pastoral counselor, motivational speaker and trainer for many organizations.

Whether it was in Africa, South America, Asia, North America or the Caribbean, it was amazing to discover that people are all the same. In the poorest village of Brazil or the wealthiest country clubhouse of the aristocracy, every human heart cries and yearns for the same thing: a chance to fulfill his or her dreams and desires. Even the poorest man has a dream. All humans possess the same desire—to be free to pursue the vision and dream in their heart.

However, for most of the over six million people on Planet Earth, this dream will end in a hopeless nightmare, not because of their lack of desire or willingness to see their dream become reality, but because of man-made circumstances and self-imposed limitations that gravitate against this desire and prevent the discovery, release and maximization of their potential. The human spirit was endowed by its Creator with the *need* to be free to pursue its purpose and to experience the fulfillment that comes with maximizing its potential. Freedom is the pursuit of the human spirit.

The word *freedom* has become common, overused and abused, like the word *love,* but little understood. Much of what we call freedom is but a corruption of our desire to have license to live without laws and accountability. The echoes of the cry for freedom are heard throughout the halls of history as individuals, generations, communities and nations seek to throw off what they perceive as restrictive yokes and burdens of oppression.

Throughout history the accounts of peoples and nations fighting and paying the ultimate price for this illusive quality give evidence of its value to the human experience. Millions have died in wars, civil unrest, uprisings and rebellions in pursuit of its promise. More human life has been sacrificed in the name of freedom than any other passion. The French Revolution was born out of the desire to throw off the yoke of monarchal oppression. The Russian Revolution was ignited by the same spark. The breaking away and formation of the Republic of the United States was fueled by the hope for freedom. The death-wish commitment of notable men like Mahatma Gandhi to see the great nation of India throw off the yoke of colonialism was propelled by the cry for freedom to determine one's own destiny. The great Civil Rights Movement of our generation, inspired by the likes of Martin Luther King, Jr., was also conceived in the womb of the desire for freedom.

Even now after entering the twenty-first century, the struggle for individual, community and national freedom continues. However, despite thousands of years of human effort to achieve an enduring and stable state of freedom, most of humanity finds itself still enslaved to bondages that hold it back and suffocates personal and national dreams. The flower children and hippies of the sixties demanded their brand of freedom, and became prisoners of the drug culture and slaves to materialism. These baby boomers produced a generation of children after their kind who fell prey to a more diabolical drug web, which strangles the life out of their purpose for life.

We now enter the age of computer technology with its promises of freedom of communication, information advancement, increased productivity and cyberspace travel over the Internet. This explosion of technological progress has rendered the twenty-first-century technocrat an overburdened fish caught in the worldwide web of confusion in an ocean of excessive information. Oh, to be free!

Why is freedom so difficult to achieve? Why does international freedom evade our experience? Why does the scientific advancement and progressive technology of our world produce more bondages than freedom? Why do we become prisoners of our own inventions and victims of our modern products? Could it be that we have misunderstood the principle of freedom? Could it be that we have confused freedom with something else?

After over forty years of study and exploration of the complex nature of human development, helping countless thousands to learn the principles and skills to improve their lives, I have come to the conclusion that the greatest pursuit in the human heart is the pursuit of freedom. The human heart has a passion to fulfill a meaningful purpose—but only a few find it.

Everyone cries for freedom and desires to be free. However, most of us who cry for freedom do not understand freedom, or the nature of liberty. It is a tragic reality that we do not understand the qualifications of true freedom. True freedom demands great responsibility, accountability, a spirit of stewardship, maturity, wisdom and character.

This book examines why freedom has become the most powerful value for mankind and why we have such an extraordinary commitment to it. Freedom is a natural concept that is foreign to most human spirits. For most of human history, and for most of the non-Western world, freedom has not been considered a value worthy of consideration or a desirable goal. Other values were and, in some cases, still are more important than freedom—values such as the pursuit of power, glory, honor, nationalism, imperial grandeur, militarism and valor in warfare, hedonism, material progress, altruism—and the list continues. But in most of these cultures, freedom was never included as a value.

In fact, most human languages did not possess a word for the concept of freedom before contact with the Western world. Japan is typical. The current Japanese word for *freedom* was only introduced during the nineteenth century when the country opened to the West.

Freedom is the central theme and value of Christianity. Being redeemed and set free from sin, bondage and fear is the goal of Christianity.

In this book, the basic perspective and argument is that freedom was generated from the experience of slavery. This includes all forms of slavery and oppression. Freedom became a principal value in human experience as a powerful, shared vision of life—a response to and result of the human experience of slavery. This oppressive spirit of slavery manifested itself in other forms such as serfdom and the roles of masters, slaves and nonslaves. In fact, slavery did not produce freedom, but rather awakened this sleeping characteristic of human nature.

The basic premise of this book is that freedom is more difficult than slavery because it demands more of us than oppression demands. We will explore the definition and misconception of freedom, and examine the nature and effects of oppression. This work addresses the concept of freedom and its implications for the individual, the community, the state and the nation. This subject will be addressed using the biblical model of the Hebrew exodus and the Israelites' transitional development from slaves throughout the creation of a sovereign free nation under the leadership of Moses and Joshua. We will discover that there is no greater burden than freedom, no heavier load than liberty. We will understand why personal freedom and national freedom are so difficult to achieve, and why oppression is so attractive. We will come to conclude that freedom, like love and beauty, is one of those values better experienced than defined. Join me on a journey to freedom.

INTRODUCTION

The person who cannot see the ultimate
becomes a slave to the immediate.

THERE IS NO greater burden than freedom, no heavier
load than liberty. The paradoxical nature of this
statement echoes the complexity of the concept of
freedom. Freedom is like beauty and love—it is
difficult to define, but you know it when you experience it. As we wade into the shallow shores of the
ocean of the twenty-first century and take on the
responsibility of custodians of a new millennium, the
cry for individual, community, cultural and national
freedom resonates from the human struggles of the
twentieth century.

Over six billion people call our fragile earth home, and
nearly everyone would claim that they are free without
any working definition of the concept. Freedom is one of
the most misunderstood ideals in human experience, and
therefore it is rarely attained. The majority of humanity

will never experience true freedom, even though freedom is the purpose and reason for man's existence.

Freedom, though little understood by most, has become the pursuit of man. Today we are living through another explosive diffusion of this ideal. The social, political and economic developments in Eastern Europe at the latter end of the twentieth century herald only the latest and most dramatic phase of the commitment of people all over the world to freedom. Since World War II, scores of countries all over the Third World and Far East have entered the struggle for freedom, embraced its value and sometimes lived by it. There is hardly a country whose leaders, however dubious, do not claim that they are pursuing the ideal of freedom. It is important to understand that the concept of freedom was not invented *by* man but *for man*. Freedom is not a Western or Eastern ideal. It is a biblical concept introduced by God Himself as the very essence and purpose of man's existence. Thus, freedom is basic to man's fulfillment and critical to his sense of value. The spirit of freedom is synonymous with the spirit of man and resides inherent in his nature. It is for this reason that the desire, passion and pursuit of freedom are natural to mankind.

Oppression, suppression and any other form of slavery or any attempt to restrict the development and expression of the human spirit will always awaken the sleeping giant called *freedom*. This is why any form of slavery, whether by forced labor, ideology, a political regime, economic oppression, domestic abuse or spiritual or religious oppression is the ultimate sin against the human spirit.

David Brion Davis and his Yale colleague Edmund Morgan, in their book *The Problem of Slavery in Western*

Culture, demonstrated the enormous importance of slavery in the social and intellectual reconstruction and reconfiguration of freedom in our modern context. Davis attempted to explain why, after taking slavery for granted since the beginning of its history in the West, in a remarkably short period of time during the late eighteenth century, slavery was redefined as the greatest evil, a moral and socioeconomic scourge that had to be exterminated. His conclusion was that the promotion and protection of personal liberty was the highest virtue of man. In essence, slavery does not destroy freedom; rather, it magnifies its presence and value. Yet the question is, What is freedom?

At the threshold of a bloody civil war, Abraham Lincoln complained that he knew no good definition of freedom. The situation is no different in our day, in spite of vast literature on the subject. In other words, while there is overwhelming agreement *on the value of liberty* ... there is a great deal of disagreement about *what freedom is*. It is this very dilemma that explains how it is possible for the most violently opposed of political parties to pay homage to the "same" ideal.

Freedom has been defined in many works of Greek philosophers, and modern thinkers and many other scholars have explored this complex subject. Freedom is defined as a tripartite value. Orlando Patterson, in his book *Freedom in the Making of Western Culture,* offers this summary:

> Freedom is a tripartite value. Freedom has a historical, sociological and conceptual relationship. There is first the concept of *personal*

freedom, which gives a person the sense that on the one hand one is not being coerced or restrained by another person in doing something desired, and on the other hand, the conviction that one can do the same.

The second concept of freedom is called *sovereign freedom.* This is simply the power to act as one pleases, regardless of the wishes of others, as distinct from personal freedom, which is the capacity to do as one pleases, in so far as one can.

The third note of freedom is *civic freedom,* which is the capacity of adult members of a community to participate in its life and governance. A person feels free, in this sense, to the degree that he or she belongs to the community of birth, has a recognized place in it, and is involved in some way in the way it is governed. The existence of civic freedom implies a political community of some sort, which clearly defines rights and obligations for every citizen. This form of freedom can still be restrictive as it was in ancient Roman culture where only male members of the community could participate, or in recent history where women or blacks were allowed to participate in the political process by the vote.[1]

These, then, are the three constitutive elements of the uniquely western chord of freedom.

However in this book we are going to look at a fourth

---

1. Orlando Patterson, *Freedom, Volume 1: Freedom in the Making of Western Culture* (n.p.: Basic Books, 1991).

concept of freedom that does not get its definition from the Greeks, the Romans or Western thinkers, but rather from the Creator of all mankind, God, and from His Word, the Bible.

This concept we will call *natural freedom*. This is freedom that exists in the very nature of man as a God-given right and responsibility established from the beginning of the creation of man. It is the human right delegated by God to man in the first book of Moses, Genesis 1:26:

> Let us make man in our image, after our likeness: and let them have *dominion* over the fish of the sea, and over the fowl of the air, and over the cattle, and over all the earth, and over every creeping thing that creepeth upon the earth.
>
> —KJV, EMPHASIS ADDED

Here in this declaration is the source and foundation of true freedom … and also the source of the very meaning of the word—*free-dominion … freedom*. True freedom is therefore "the liberty to dominate the earth through one's unique gifts and talents in fulfillment of God's purpose for one." In essence, each individual was created by God to dominate the environment through his or her personal gifts and talents, in pursuit of fulfilling God's personal purpose for his or her life and to serve others with that purpose. Freedom is the liberty to fulfill God's will in serving others with the gift of that purpose, without restricting or controlling another while that person fulfills his or her purpose and serves you.

It is also important to note that God's instructions specify what man is to dominate and not dominate.

Man is conspicuously missing from the list. True freedom is self-discovery of one's personal purpose and the liberty to pursue the fulfillment of that purpose according to the laws and principles established by God, without restricting others from doing the same. In this definition, the most important implication is that of personal responsibility.

This definition naturally establishes the fact that any domination of another human spirit is violation of God's natural law. This will be our working definition of freedom in this book. Who are the first people in every generation to get the idea that being free is not only a value to be cherished but also the most important thing that someone could possess? The answer, in a word, is slaves. Freedom normally begins to manifest itself as a social value in the desperate yearning of the slave to negate what, for him or her and for nonslaves, is a peculiarly inhumane condition. This is because freedom is not the creation of a new social status given as a privilege to the disadvantaged, but rather a natural restoration to the normal state of what it means to be man.

To fully understand freedom, we must have a better knowledge of the condition called slavery. As Orlando Patterson states:

> Slavery is the permanent, violent and personal domination of natally alienated and generally dishonored persons. It is first a form of personal domination. One individual is under the direct power of another or his agent. In practice, this usually entails the power of life and death over the

6

slave. Second, the slave is always an excommunicated person. He or she does not belong to the legitimate social or moral community; he has no independent social existence; he exists only through, and for, the master; he is natally alienated. Third, the slave is in a perpetual condition of dishonor. What is more, the master and his group parasitically gain honor in degrading the slave.[2]

No discussion of freedom will be complete without a clear understanding of the nature of slavery. This specter of slavery is not only limited to physical oppression, but is also true of spiritual slavery and oppression. The biblical concept is that of the human race falling under the slave yoke of the prince of darkness as a result of the rebellion and disobedience of man's forefather, Adam. The impact of slavery is the same in every circumstance, whether spiritual, mental or physical, whether individual, cultural, community or national slavery. Any attempt to limit, control, hinder, restrict, inhibit, prevent or stop the fulfillment of God's purpose and will in another's life is rebellion against God. This is called *wickedness. Rebellion* is identified as the sin of witchcraft, which is defined as any attempt to control the will and spirit of another. In every case of oppression, the cry for freedom is eminent.

The impact of slavery is not limited to the physical damage it can wreak on the slave, but to the more diabolical mental damage it causes. This is the most tragic element of slavery—both physical and spiritual. In fact,

2. Ibid.

the goal of the oppressor is mental slavery. This is called *breaking the spirit*. This is the surrender of hope in the human spirit, and is the most dangerous aspect of oppression.

When oppression becomes a mental condition, then physical freedom is not enough. It is this crucial principle that this book will address. The mind is the key to life. "As [a man] thinketh in his heart [mind], so is he" (Prov. 23:7, KJV). *Therefore, your mental state is more important than your physical state. You are not free until your mind is liberated. Freedom is first a mental condition before it is a physical statement.* This is the basis for the statement made by the ultimate man, the Prince of peace, the source of true freedom—Jesus Christ—when He presented His proposition on freedom as recorded by His disciple in John 8:32: "Then you will know the truth, and the truth will set you free." The source of freedom, according to Jesus, is not legislation or a key to a chain, but rather knowledge—the discovery of information powerful enough to set you free in your mind. If a man is what he thinks, then a man is not free until he thinks free.

Therefore, it is possible to be delivered and yet not be free. Deliverance is physical liberation from physical restrictions. Deliverance is the removal of the oppressed from the environment of the oppressor. Deliverance is the separation of the slave from the physical conditions of slavery. One of the major causes of frustration and disillusionment in the human experience, especially among those who have been victims of historical oppression and abuse, is their confusing deliverance with freedom. Deliverance is not freedom. Deliverance *prepares* you for freedom.

Many nations who were forged in the fires of oppression and emerged from the dust of colonialism and slavery are still struggling, after many years of independence, to find the trophy of true freedom. Some who have mistaken deliverance for freedom continue to stagger under the power of mental slavery. Some have even passed this oppressive mentality on to the next generation. How does the individual, the community and the nation break this spirit of mental oppression and move on to freedom?

To answer this question, we will study the model established by the Creator, who produced a prototype in the case of delivering a band of Hebrew slaves from the oppressive power of the Egyptian Pharaoh and moved them through the process of the wilderness to the land of promise, making them a sovereign free nation. A careful study of this excellent model provides us, as individuals, communities or nations, with the principles necessary to move from slavery to deliverance and to our destiny of freedom to fulfill God's purpose for our lives.

We must learn that freedom is not the absence of law, work or labor, but the embracing of responsibility. We must be awakened to the reality that true freedom imposes more laws than slavery, demands more work than slavery and demands more self-control and discipline than slavery. The foundation of true freedom is management—self-management and management of our environment. This is the first and ultimate purpose of God for mankind. In slavery you do not manage—you are managed. Therefore,

freedom is a return to the responsibility of stewardship. God's first command to man was to manage the
real estate called Earth. Man was given the management contract to manage the earth, and his freedom is
inherent in this dominion mandate. You are not free
until you are able to dominate an area of earth with
your gift. I challenge you to read the following pages
with an open heart and to experience the freedom
awaiting you in the land of promise—the land of milk,
honey and responsibility.

The price of greatness is responsibility.
—Winston Churchill

ONE

THE PROMISE OF TRUE FREEDOM

**The God who gave us life gave us
liberty at the same time.**

—*THOMAS JEFFERSON*

REEDOM IS A burden that only the mature can bear. It happens in our minds as we accept our responsibility to move forward and allow the reconditioning of our oppressive thinking. Those who won't move forward travel in aimless wilderness circles, because nothing truly changes until your mind changes.

I read a report in a science journal recently about a scientist who was studying the power of conditioning. This scientist's team leashed a dog to a stake. Then they put the animal's food just out of reach. When the dog tried to get the food, he hurt himself because his leash wasn't long enough. Every time he lunged toward the food, he felt pain.

By the fourth week of this cruel experiment, the dog stayed right by the stake. He didn't even try to reach for the food. During the fifth week they removed the dog's leash and put him two feet away from the food. But by now the dog stayed next to the stake. The animal refused to go near the food. He had been so conditioned by the pain that kept him from reaching the food that, although he was free to eat again, he believed he couldn't.

That dog almost starved to death during the last seven weeks of his testing. He wouldn't move from the stake even though the food was accessible. They actually had to pick the dog up and carry him to the food to slowly recondition him.

This experiment, cruel as it was, demonstrated that when the mind of an animal is conditioned, it will live within the limitations imposed upon it even after it is set free. It also clearly illustrates the problem God had with the children of Israel. They were in slavery, tied to Pharaoh's stake of bondage for 430 years. Then one day God sent a man named Moses to remove the leash and deliver them. And he did deliver Israel from the hand of their oppressor. But delivering them from their oppressed way of thinking was another thing.

The reason God refused to take the Israelites directly into Canaan following their deliverance was because they were still mentally enslaved in Egypt. They had been delivered from Egypt, but they weren't yet free. So God had to deal with their minds, though their bodies were already liberated from bondage. This illustration captures a principle that applies to individuals, communities and nations: *Conditions determine conduct until interrupted by an external force.*

The major component missing in the life of most believers and Christian communities is the knowledge base of management. It is toward the end of changing this situation that I have written the following chapters. We have not learned to harness the irresponsibility handed down from Adam and have misunderstood and mismanaged our calling to rule the earth. To so many of us, heaven is the objective and oppression is our mind-set. Like the Hebrews of old we are marching in circles, unaware of the good life on earth. In the meantime, we can speak in tongues, but we can't speak to the banker. We can jump and dance "in the Spirit," but we can't manage our own lives.

Some so-called successful Christians who have positions and titles in companies can't manage their own families. They're making $600,000 a year, but they're wandering around in the wilderness when it comes to loving their spouse. They have learned to manage and earn money, but they can't manage their homes. Psalm 127:1 says, "Unless the LORD builds the house, its builders labor in vain." In this book I want to address management God's way—which makes everyone whole.

To achieve my goals of instruction, I will be using some illustrations from the business world to make some management points. We will also discuss the negative—what "not to do"—in some aspects to accentuate the positive. And we will let Israel's historic exodus from Egypt serve as redirective teaching points. The end result will hopefully be a management cap that fits perfectly around your Christian crown.

CREATED FOR FREEDOM

FREEDOM—WHAT IT is and what it's not—is the core principle of Adam's original relationship and the purpose of this book. In the Genesis account, God, the Creator, placed the man in the Garden and said, "You are free."

> And the LORD God commanded the man, *"You are free* to eat from any tree in the garden; but you must not eat from the tree of the knowledge of good and evil, for when you eat of it you will surely die."
>
> —GENESIS 2:16–17, EMPHASIS ADDED

God declared man free and gave him work. Freedom is basic to God's will for man. Adam was free to produce, duplicate, multiply and replenish everything God had given him to do, but he wasn't free to violate the law of God. God put just one item in the Garden to maintain man's obedience—the tree of the knowledge of good and evil. Imagine the millions of trees God had made, yet He placed a "No Trespassing" sign in front of just one of them. This was necessary in order to activate the will of man through the power of choice.

DELIVERANCE IS NOT FREEDOM

YOU MAY HAVE built a nice little homestead on the edge of Sinai's wilderness. You have become comfortable in your oppression, but you know there is so much more that God has in store for you. You've given up on miracles because you don't see them anymore. You haven't been listening to the mentors assigned to your life. And you haven't been faithful to God's Word. You've been delivered, but you aren't living free. Still, you know there's more to this life. That's why I'm writing to you.

There is no way to walk into freedom without shouldering its responsibility. If you want that promotion to general manager, you must want the position's responsibility. The price of responsibility requires more time, talent, energy, initiative and substance. The title is nice, and the pay is wonderful, but the workload is sevenfold. You have to be there earlier than everyone else and be the last one to leave when you are in charge. If anything goes wrong, they call you—day or night. If the water pipe bursts at 3 A.M., get ready for a phone call. The nine-to-five work day doesn't apply to you anymore, because now *you're* the general manager, and now *you* work all the time.

It's easy to be a janitor, because you can leave at five. When you're working as a clerk, you can sometimes slip out for a two-hour lunch, and nobody cares too much. But if you ever want to progress, you will have to grow up into the responsibility of freedom, because there is a cost to being free.

Being released from the oppressor does not guarantee a release from oppression—responsibility does. Responsibility makes the hard-working choices to get up earlier and work into the night to get the job done. And this is what freedom allows us to do when we honestly want to be truly free.

Are You Sitting by the Door?

WHEN JESUS BEGAN His ministry, He stood in the synagogue at Nazareth and read from the Book of Isaiah: "The Spirit of the Lord is on me, because he has anointed me to preach good news to the poor. He has sent me to proclaim freedom for the prisoners and recovery of sight for the blind, to release the oppressed, to proclaim the year of the Lord's favor" (Luke 4:18–19).

The terminology used in this passage paints a picture of someone who visits a prison and finds all the doors are opened, but the prisoners are still inside. Jesus said He came to *proclaim* freedom to the prisoners. The prison doors were open, but the prisoners were still sitting inside. They were glad, like so many individuals and nations today, that the door of deliverance was open. They were proud the door was open. But they were still sitting inside on their prison cots. Why? Because prisons provide free food. When you're in jail, your clothes are paid for. Showers are provided, and you can sit and watch the world move around you on cable TV.

I've actually met young people who have told me, "I do better in prison than on the outside; at least I know I'll get three square meals a day behind bars. I have a job in prison. I know who I am in prison—I'm a prisoner. Out here I don't know who I am." How sad.

Too many people are wasting their time today as prisoners in their own cells. Christ's words of freedom may be taped to their living room walls. But so many are sitting in their cells with the jail door standing wide open, enslaved to the spirit of oppression that held them bound before accepting deliverance.

The word *gospel* means "good news, good report, good herald or good information." *The good news of the kingdom is that Jesus converts our deliverance into freedom.* When a man is born again, the Spirit of God re-creates his inner man and makes His abode in him. But the freedom that comes to our mind and actions is left completely up to us. We are *free* to walk out of our jail cells, and we are *free* to stay in our cells, because according to Christ's gospel, no one is automatically *set* free. In your oppression you have chosen to sit in your jail cell and watch TV. You bought that VCR, and now your new church is the video store.

The great Jewish apostle Paul writes, "It is for freedom that Christ has set us free. Stand firm, then, and do not let yourselves be burdened again by a yoke of slavery" (Gal. 5:1).

As the church, nations and individuals travel the road to responsibility today, it is important to understand that many of us have been conditioned by our former oppression. Our social, economic and religious conditioning ties us to an invisible stake (like the dog in the experiment), which keeps us from moving forward in the things of God. The jail cell is open, but there we sit, bound and oppressed. This is why Paul tells us to stand firm against the conditioning to renew our minds from our old ways of thinking.

GET RID OF THE OLD THINKING

WHEN I WAS growing up, we lived in a part of the Bahamas that wasn't economically desirable. Then one year our family built a new house on the east side of Nassau in an area that everybody was dreaming of moving to at that time.

Before we moved, thirteen of us—eleven children plus a mother and a father—were living in a little four-room house. Things were so confusing at times that my brother and I used to wear each other's socks. When we were getting ready to move into our newly constructed house in the promised land, I remember my mother saying, "You all can't act up there like you act down here." That sounds simple, but she was imparting a deep revelation: "Look, we are moving to a new place, so we need new children." There was a water pump outside of our old house that had to be primed and pumped every morning when starting our day. That was a tough job. I used to hate to prime the pump. My arms ached as I longed to be eating breakfast or getting some more rest.

When it was time to bathe, we had to pump water into a bucket, carry it into the house and pour it into a tin tub. Each one of us got into that tin tub and stood up so Mama could bathe us. Every morning it was pump, pour and shiver in the cold well water that started out our day.

When we crossed over into our promised land, the pumping and pouring was a thing of the past. Now we had running water inside the house. But we still had our old wilderness "tin tub" mentality. We had a brand-new porcelain tub, but we didn't know how to bathe in it! We stood up in the new tub just like we used to stand up in that tin tub; it took years to realize that we could actually lie down to take a bath.

This may seem a funny little illustration, but you see, we had been conditioned just like that dog. We were in a new land, but mentally we were still in the old place. *Position does not guarantee disposition.*

In the old house we used to wash the dishes in a basin. Imagine the dishes for eleven children plus mom and dad—thirteen plates, thirteen forks, thirteen knives, thirteen cups, thirteen everything. It was like a hotel. We used to pile up the dishes in an enamel basin and wash them. Then we would place them in a rubber tub so they could drip dry.

When we moved to the promised land, we had a new built-in sink, but instead of letting the dishes dry in the sink, we put them in the old rubber tub. It took a little time to realize we had a sink—and what it was for! *So "new" does not guarantee change.*

GOOD-BYE, EGYPT!

NOW HERE IS the point: When some folks move from Egypt, they carry their old washboards with them. When they arrive in Canaan, they carry those old washboards into the laundromat, put them in a new Whirlpool or GE electric washing machine and scrub away. They don't even question the strange, new wash tubs with open lids and shiny dials. The electronic wonders are staring them in the face, but they have been so conditioned in slavery that they don't even question what the new things are.

This is a good illustration of being delivered, but not free. Washing machines clean clothing at the flip of a button. With them, scraped fingers and sore arms are things of the past. But when the past consumes your present, it makes no difference. The laundromat becomes just a new place to do what you did at the river the year before. This is the kind of oppressive thinking that God wants out of us. Of course it's tough to change—*without mental transformation, the actions we take to "change" may only produce a new place where we continue to do our old things.*

There are millions today who are tied to a stake or scrubbing in laundromats because the oppressive conditioning of their past is still controlling their present. Many have been conditioned to say, "I can't be holy; I am a worm, hoping for heaven. I hope I make it, because I certainly can't be righteous on earth. What are we having for dinner in the prison cafeteria today? I can't be myself. I can't be delivered. I can't be healed. I can't be liberated. I can't be free." They're so used to believing those lies that when God tells them they are free, they can't believe it's true. They sit in their prison cells, simply hearing the good news of freedom in the gospel, but they don't believe it.

Millions are bound by their past. Though their chains have been removed, they are so bound by the lies of Egypt's conditioning that they never walk out into freedom to enjoy the fruits of their destiny. *The comfort of having others control their lifestyle in slavery is too appealing for many.* So they hang around the stake, starving. They don't exercise their minds, and they never learn what is outside of their comfortable prison doors.

The twenty-first-century message of the Creator is this: *Obedience demands responsibility to walk out of our prison doors.* We have wandered in the wilderness naming and claiming long enough. Our free ride is over. It's time to get to work!

RENEW YOUR MIND

As AMAZING AS it sounds, the one thing God could not do with the Hebrew children in the wilderness was to change their minds. And He can't change yours, either. He will inspire you in your godly desires, but He won't change you. *The only one who can change you is you.* This is why the apostle Paul wrote in his letter to the Christian church at Rome, "Do not conform any longer to the pattern of this world, but be transformed by the renewing of your mind" (Rom. 12:2).

Remember what my mother taught us before we moved into our new modern house? "You all have to

20

change." The word *transformed* used by Paul in this verse in Romans means "changed." But that has nothing to do with our spirits. Spiritual transformation takes place when we are born again. When we change kingdoms, our spirits are renewed. I compare the new birth change of kingdoms to the move my family made from our little four-room house to our new deluxe home on the east side of our island.

> He has rescued us from the dominion of darkness and brought us into the kingdom of the Son he loves.
>
> —Colossians 1:13

All things were new when we moved in; the old had passed away. But once we arrived, our thinking remained the same. *It is the mind that must be renewed before we can walk out of oppression's chains.*

The trouble is that when we are born again in our spirit, we still have our washboard in our hands. We're still carrying all this weight. We still have old thinking patterns with us. Our minds need to be renewed.

We never had any lawn at our old home. We just had dirt. When we arrived at our new home we had grass. Grass is better than dirt, don't you think? But I'll never forget how angry I became the first week we were there because I couldn't shoot marbles on our nice new lawn. You need dirt to shoot marbles, but instead of planning to shoot somewhere else, because of my old-house oppressive thinking, I was angry at the grass! I was angry because I couldn't play my old games in the new place.

You can't play the old wilderness games in the land of

Canaan. They don't work there. Are you still a player? If you are, you need a conversion in your soul.

The soul consists of the mind, will and emotions. *Nothing changes until the soul changes.* It is God's law—His living active written truth—that converts the soul. Have you ever heard the expression "A man is what he eats"? How about the term "soul food"? Both of these phrases are pregnant with wisdom and contain the key to change and freedom. *What you feed your soul determines your quality of life and degree of freedom.*

> The law of the LORD is perfect, converting the soul.
> —PSALM 19:7, KJV

The Book of Hebrews tells us, "For the word of God is living and active. Sharper than any double-edged sword, it penetrates even to *dividing soul and spirit,* joints and marrow; it judges the thoughts and attitudes of the heart" (Heb. 4:12, emphasis added). The soul is separate from man's spirit, which is re-created at the new birth. The soul is called *psuche* in biblical Greek and refers to "the seat of the feelings, desires, affections, aversions."

The apostle James writes, "Therefore lay aside all filthiness and overflow of wickedness, and receive with meekness the implanted word, which is able to save your souls" (James 1:21, NKJV).

Change comes through mental reconditioning after a person is born again. So it is up to every individual to save his soul after his spirit has been born again. If you don't, you will lie by the same old stake and sit in the same old cell that your carnal mind conditioned you for before you were born again. *Every one of us must renew and retrain our minds for freedom.*

Have you ever made or heard this statement, "I need a change"? In response to this, many make a geographical, physical move (sometimes internationally), change jobs and even spouses, only to discover they are still frustrated. Why? Because change comes not by where we go, but through what we know. Transformation begins with information. If you truly want to change, change your library, friends and influences.

DELIVERED SPIRITS WITH OPPRESSED MINDS

THE WAY A person thinks about himself is a key to how he will think about others and to his general outlook on life. Certain people could move into your neighborhood and bring the property values down. If they moved next door to your $200,000 house and treated theirs like it was a $50,000 home, all of a sudden your home's value would start dropping.

When the realtor drives by and sees the uncut grass, weeds and trash covering their lawn, the realtor will think twice, attempting to cut your sale price because of your trash-thinking neighbor. The realtor will say, "We need to take an extra $7,000 off the sale price to help the buyer endure the unsightly house next door."

Do you know what is God's number one problem on the planet? It is humans with delivered spirits but the same old oppressed minds. He has to put up with old trashy minds in a new and holy kingdom, and we bring God's value down by our bad attitudes and by the way we treat ourselves and others.

God knew He couldn't take the Israelites directly

into freedom when Moses delivered them, because they would have turned Canaan into Egypt. So He took the time to work on their minds. Those whose minds He couldn't change, He later buried in the wilderness.

Only people who are mature, willing to fight and willing to take responsibility for the future are going to bear fruit for God in the new millennium. I believe we are going to bury some wilderness people because they are not ready for the awesome responsibility that lies ahead of us. They will still be naming and claiming or sitting and doing nothing, and when God stops answering their baby prayers, they'll think He left. Then they will murmur and die in the wilderness just as the Israelites did. He is going to wake a lot of these folks up. But some of them will have spiritually deaf ears.

It takes free minds and a lot of guts to face Jericho. You need some backbone to look at the Amorite kings and declare, "We're going to defeat you." It takes a lot of internal fortitude to stand back and tell Joshua, "We can well take the land." *It is easier to exist in slavery than to live in freedom.* This is why many individuals, communities and nations who have experienced the excitement of deliverance turn their celebration into criticism when the reality of responsibility confronts them.

FREE MINDS

THERE IS A situation recorded in the writings of the apostle Paul to the Roman metropolitan city of Corinth that illustrates the struggle to be truly free.

Some Christians in Paul's day experienced the same kind of Egypt-thinking problems in the New Testament promised land of the church as Israel did in the wilderness. Many of the Greek Christians were idol worshipers before they came to the Lord. After they were saved they realized there was only one God, but a problem arose. The idolatrous thinking from the past threatened their new Christian lifestyle. So Paul wrote these words to them:

> So then, about eating food sacrificed to idols: We know that an idol is nothing at all in the world and that there is no God but one.... For us there is but one God, the Father, from whom all things came and for whom we live; and there is but one Lord, Jesus Christ, through whom all things came and through whom we live. But not everyone knows this. Some people are still so accustomed to idols that when they eat such food they think of it as having been sacrificed to an idol, and since their conscience is weak, it is defiled.
>
> —1 Corinthians 8:4–7

Paul knew that meat sacrificed to idols meant nothing because the "gods" to whom it was sacrificed didn't exist. But some of the new Corinthian Christians had been so conditioned by their past that they were afraid to eat meat that had been offered to their culture's mythical gods. Their oppressive past affected their present, and they allowed the practice to affect their new freedom.

Other Corinthian Christians grew in their understanding of God's soul-restoring truth and had no problem eating "pagan-brand" meats. But because of the dangers of oppressive thinking, which can kill God's people in the wilderness, Paul warned the Corinthians:

Be careful, however, that the exercise of your freedom does not become a stumbling block to the weak. For if anyone with a weak conscience sees you who have this knowledge eating in an idol's temple, won't he be emboldened to eat what has been sacrificed to idols? So this weak brother, for whom Christ died, is destroyed by your knowledge. When you sin against your brothers in this way and wound their weak conscience, you sin against Christ. Therefore, if what I eat causes my brother to fall into sin, I will not eat meat again, so that I will not cause him to fall.

—1 CORINTHIANS 8:9–13

Paul calls the people who were offended by eating meat sacrificed to idols "brethren" because they were saved, born-again people. They had the Holy Spirit. The problem was, they were still oppressed by their old pagan life. So when they saw meat that they used to offer to idols, they still saw the idols with the meat. They had been delivered from that old culture and lifestyle, but they weren't free in their thinking to progress spiritually.

Our former idols today don't usually consist of wood and stone idols. An idol may be a former hobby that God wants you to cut down on to give Him more time. Or it may be a habit you gave up that keeps trying to come back. If you aren't free in your mind after conversion, even your eating can become bondage. *When you are free, your mind needs to be free with you.*

Paul declared his own freedom late in 1 Corinthians. But he also acknowledged that he would back down from that freedom if it would prevent others from sinning.

26

"Though I am free and belong to no man, I make myself a slave to everyone, to win as many as possible" (9:19). In his freedom, Paul put serving others above his own desires. He went where the oppressed people were and, through the truth, delivered them into freedom. There is no true freedom without responsibility.

LET THE PAST PASS

WHEN GOD DELIVERED the Israelites from Egypt, He gave them the opportunity to be free. But they refused the opportunity. So God buried them in the desert, and He used their children, who were not born in Egypt, to possess the land instead.

Deliverance provides the *opportunity* for freedom, not the *fulfillment* of freedom. The jail door is opened, but you must choose to walk out. Once you hit the wilderness, watch out with whom you're hanging out. If you keep company with Egypt-thinking people, they can contaminate you. It was for this reason that God didn't allow the childrens' parents to circumcise them. God didn't want this new generation to bear a mark that was made by their slave-minded fathers. He didn't want any memory of Egypt to remind them of slavery's past.

> The Israelites had moved about in the desert forty years until all the men who were of military age when they left Egypt had died, since they had not obeyed the LORD. For the LORD had sworn to them that they would not see the land that he had solemnly promised their fathers to give us, a land flowing with milk and honey. *So he raised up*

27

their sons in their place, and these were the ones Joshua circumcised.

—JOSHUA 5:6–7, EMPHASIS ADDED

I sit down and talk with older people sometimes, but there are certain ones with whom I'm careful about talking. There are some who only talk about how they were oppressed. Some can talk about it for hours. And if you sit there and listen, a hatred can develop in you for a people you don't even know. *So be careful; the oppressive past of others can contaminate your spirit and inhibit your true freedom.*

I highly value the talk of old people who say, "Son, appreciate what you have, because we didn't have this." To me, that's gratefulness. That's an encouragement to be appreciative of what God is doing in your life.

But I am very careful about others who say, "I remember when we couldn't eat in the same restaurant with those scoundrels who controlled our land. We couldn't go here, or go there. We knew our place, because they told us where it was!" These are the ones who can pass along their hatred, and it can become a cancer to you.

We can become so preoccupied with the realities of the past that our present and future can be consumed. *Some people are so busy trying to get over their past that they don't have time to live their future.* Paul tells us to forget those things that are behind, and that "straining toward what is ahead, I press on toward the goal to win the prize for which God has called me heavenward in Christ Jesus" (Phil. 3:13).

To this, God adds in Isaiah 43, "Forget the former things; do not dwell on the past. See, I am doing a new thing!" (vv. 18–19). This does not mean we are to pretend that the past did not exist. We must simply not allow it to control, inhibit or condemn our future.

This is a powerful word to the church of the twenty-first century. Today we are embarking on a whole new era for the church. But to get on with God's leading we must look at our lives and make a responsible decision to "forget the former things." We can't preoccupy ourselves with the way we were or the way we were treated, because it only produces bitterness. We must consider any past grievances as the works of ignorant people, forgive and move on. *The past is as strong as you allow it to be.* To the Israelites, the scent of onions and garlic became stronger than their desire for sweet honey and milk.

This is a basic issue of spiritual salvation. To get saved, you have to turn your back on *where* you were going and *whom* you were with and go totally *in the other direction.* You can't look back to the wilderness or to Egypt. Those good old miracle days of the Charismatic movement are gone. We are whooping, shouting, dancing and falling down out of tradition, because the anointing is gone. But God hasn't left. He just wants to do a new thing. So don't look back. As Jesus said, "No one who puts his hand to the plow and looks back is fit for service in the kingdom of God" (Luke 9:62). God has a higher level of responsibility for your life. But you must forget what is behind you to progress in your calling. You can't take hold of the new without first letting go of the old.

Delivered but Not Free

When Jesus called you, He didn't just call you to save you.

29

He called you so you could be free. "You, my brothers," writes Paul again, "were called to be free" (Gal. 5:13). Paul is talking in this verse to saints, which indicates they were saved—but not free. We all have to respond to our freedom call because of the reality of remaining bound by the spirit of oppression after we have been born again.

This is a timely message for the church today, because it's time to grow up. We can actually be born again and remain unborn in our minds. So the apostle writes again, "Do not use your freedom to indulge the sinful nature; rather, serve one another in love" (Gal. 5:13).

In other words, Paul tells us, "Don't use your freedom to indulge in 'Egyptian living.'" *Some of us are glad to be delivered from the oppressor, but we don't want deliverance from the oppression.* We are excited to be saved, but we know those areas of our mind that need to be renewed—and we like to hold on to them. "God, I'm so glad You redeemed me, but don't redeem me from those other things. You know I still like to sip a bit in the Pharaoh Bar and Grill. You know I'm busy, and I can't get this together with my weight, and I still like to hang out with those old mummies down the street. Let all of my freedom from them come when it's time to hit heaven's gates." So there some sit in their little homesteads on the edge of the Sinai wilderness, visiting with old friends, in sight of the Promised Land.

Listen: The people of Israel really didn't want to go back to Pharaoh. They wanted to go back to the food. They hated Pharaoh, but they loved what he offered them—free food, free housing, free clothes. So in essence, they said, "Deliver us, but don't set us free from this stuff."

30

Get the Stink Out

Just as God called the Israelites, He is calling you to be free. It's time to grow up. It's time to cut off all that Egyptian scent. Get up off your jail cot and bathe yourself in the blood one more time. Put down those old smelly Cairo leek-and-onion sandwiches you've been secretly eating, and wash yourself in the fresh truth of God's Word. Get all the garlic scent out of your system. Go on a long fast if you can. Get the onions and leeks out of your blood.

While driving to church a while back I picked up a young man who used to attend our ministry in Nassau. He was flagging a ride—and was he shocked that I was the one who stopped for him.

"How are you doing, son?" I asked.

"Hi, Pastor. N-n-not too good."

"What do you mean, 'Not too good'?"

"You know, I mean, you know...I haven't been around the church, and I've been wandering off." Already he had started repenting.

"I know I'm doing things that I know I shouldn't...."

"It's OK," I said. "You don't have to tell me anything. I can smell it. Man, you smell like Egypt."

When I dropped him off, I said, "Let's pray."

"Right here?" he asked.

"Yes, right here," I said, "with everybody watching. Let's pray right here. I want to pray for you."

I prayed, "Lord, You delivered him, now set him free." Then I told him that he had to make a decision to seek God's freedom in his life. Witnessing wouldn't help him, because he already knew the good Word of

God and had drunk of His Spirit. He had already been delivered, but now he had to make a decision to act responsibly in his freedom. He alone was responsible for his own future, so he had to choose.

The worldwide church is currently on the outskirts of the wilderness. We can hear the Jordan rushing along just over the hill. We are at the end of our generation, and we are moving into the Promised Land. So it is time to learn how to walk in our freedom. It's time to stop playing our games and to break away from the chains that hold us to our stakes. Let us move on now to learn more about walking in freedom.

> Injustice anywhere is a threat to justice everywhere.
>
> —MARTIN LUTHER KING, JR.

PRINCIPLES OF FREEDOM

CHAPTER 1
THE PROMISE OF TRUE FREEDOM

1. Conditions determine conduct until interrupted by an external force.
2. There is no way to walk into freedom without shouldering its responsibility.
3. Being released from the oppressor does not guarantee a release from oppression—responsibility does.
4. The good news of the kingdom is that Jesus converts our deliverance into freedom.
5. Position does not guarantee disposition.
6. "New" does not guarantee change.
7. Without mental transformation, the actions we take to "change" may only produce a new place where we continue to do our old things.
8. The comfort of having others control their lifestyle in slavery is too appealing for many.
9. Obedience demands responsibility to walk out of our prison doors.
10. The only one who can change you is you.
11. It is the mind that must be renewed before we can walk out of oppression's chains.
12. You can't play the old wilderness games in the land of Canaan.
13. Nothing changes until the soul changes.
14. What you feed your soul determines your quality of life and degree of freedom.
15. Every one of us must renew and retrain our minds for freedom.
16. Only people who are mature, willing to fight and willing to take responsibility for the future are going to bear fruit for God in the new millennium.
17. It is easier to exist in slavery than to live in freedom.
18. When you are free, your mind needs to be free with you.
19. Be careful—the oppressive past of others can contaminate your spirit and inhibit your true freedom.
20. Some people are so busy trying to get over their past that they don't have time to live their future.
21. The past is as strong as you allow it to be.
22. Some of us are glad to be delivered from the oppressor, but we don't want deliverance from the oppression.

TWO

FALLING SHORT
OF FREEDOM'S PROMISE

No one is more dangerous than a
mountain man with a valley mentality.

WHEN MY WIFE, Ruth, and I traveled to Egypt, we were amazed at how short the flight was from Israel to Egypt. It seemed as if we had no sooner lifted off in our plane than we were landing, and I actually thought we had touched down in some intermediary place. But after we landed in Cairo and I realized that I had been looking down at the Sinai Desert and Israel both at the same time, I thought, *Wait a minute—forty years?! It took Israel forty years to get from here to there?!*

During a tour of the hot desert area where the ancient Israelites wandered in the pursuit of freedom, we learned that it would have taken only thirty-five days to walk into Israel. The Israelites were only a month away from servitude to statehood.

Ruth and I were amazed at how little had changed along the Nile since the pharaohs ruled supremely throughout the ancient world. Bricks are still made of straw and mud, just as they were when scaffolds surrounded the mighty Sphinx.

Throughout our journey I continued to reflect on how short the distance was that this historic band of Semitic refugees actually had to walk. In this light, the magnitude of the fledgling nation's rebellion takes on a new perspective. Let's review the story.

The twelve tribes of the Hebrew patriarch Jacob began as free men and women, enjoying the great wealth and prosperity that freedom can bring. They relocated to Egypt to escape a worldwide famine. In Egypt, they fell under the direction of Jacob's youngest son, Joseph, who had risen to the office of prime minister in Pharaoh's court. When Joseph and Pharaoh died, Pharaoh's successor, Ramses I, made slaves of the mushrooming mass of foreigners. Exodus 1:9–11 tells us:

> "Look," he said to his people, "the Israelites have become much too numerous for us. Come, we must deal shrewdly with them or they will become even more numerous and, if war breaks out, will join our enemies, fight against us and leave the country." So they put slave masters over them to oppress them with forced labor, and they built Pithom and Rameses as store cities for Pharaoh.

The Book of Exodus also introduces the famous Hebrew deliverer Moses. Drawn from the waters of the Nile in the papyrus basket by Pharaoh's daughter, Moses was raised in the trappings of royalty. We learn little about Moses' life until the time when he committed a murder and fled into Midian, where he

35

prepared for leadership as a shepherd for forty years.

Moses experienced an astounding encounter with God at Mt. Sinai's burning bush, and Israel's long-awaited deliverer was called forth from obscurity. The time was right, and God embarked on the Bible's historic account of relocating these former slaves, under the leadership of Moses, into their famous Promised Land of Canaan—a month-long journey by foot. Nevertheless, it took them forty years to walk the distance.

A LONG WALK TO NOWHERE

THE ISRAELITES TOOK a long walk to nowhere. The Bible also says that when God delivered these people, He took them on a longer route, bypassing Philistine country to keep them from changing their minds.

> When Pharaoh let the people go, God did not lead them on the road through the Philistine country, though that was shorter. For God said, "If they face war, *they might change their minds* and return to Egypt."
>
> —EXODUS 13:17, EMPHASIS ADDED

See what the sovereign Creator of the universe was actually concerned about here. "If these people face war," God was literally saying, "they will change their minds and want to return to Egypt. Their slave mentality could reject My promise. So we must avoid the encounter." Now this is truly astounding. After all the amazing miracles and supernatural manifestations God worked to deliver these people, He understood their earthly thinking could still thwart His redemptive plan.

You know, coming from the Caribbean, I can relate

at least partially to ancient Israel's mind-set. These people had been slaves in Egypt for 430 years. My own Caribbean nation had been under British rule for 250 years. So we know what it is like to live under the thumb of a foreign power. Many of my countrymen continue to suffer today from some of the leftover ways of thinking that held us as captives.

Israel was protected by the oppressor when they lived in oppression. My nation understands this. Israel was not a warring people. Neither is mine. The majority of my ancestors in the Bahamas were taken as slaves from West Africa to farm British land in the Caribbean. Israel's people were conditioned to be servants, and so were we. We were marched out to the sugar cane fields until British slavery was abolished in 1827. Then we were treated as second-class citizens until our national independence from colonialism was officially ratified in 1973. Remember, moving to another city, country or continent may change your circumstances, but it doesn't change you.

The Hebrews had been servants and forced laborers under the thumb of the Egyptians for so long that servitude evolved as their national heritage. Their lives were strictly controlled, and their days were spent making bricks to build Egypt's fine houses and famous pyramids. They also constructed Egypt's aqueducts for irrigation, and they farmed wheat and corn in the desert. But none of it was their own. They were told what to do, when to do it and where to do it every day of their lives for more than four hundred years. When God's redemptive clock struck the hour of their deliverance, the Hebrews couldn't handle it, and a one-month walk to freedom turned into a forty-year sojourn to nowhere.

As a Man Thinks in His Heart, So Is He

You are made *of the sum total of the choices and decisions you make every day.* Once the Hebrews were free from their Egyptian oppressors, God made Israel's decisions and worked mighty miracles for them during their exodus in order to fulfill His sovereign will. But the will of Israel was another thing. The Israelites were used to others doing their thinking for them, and when times got tough, like a broken record they bitterly complained—"We want to go back to Egypt! We want to go home! We remember the fish we ate in Egypt at no cost—also the cucumbers, melons, leeks, onions and garlic" (Num. 11:5).

Wandering in the Desert of Underachievement

It took God forty years to reeducate Moses in the shepherd fields of Midian before he was prepared to take up his divine appointment as Israel's deliverer. Moses would soon learn the hard way that the most difficult job in the world is the reeducation and reconstruction of other potential deliverers. King Solomon tells us in Proverbs 23:7, "As [a man] thinks in his heart, so is he" (NKJV). And the Hebrews *thought* they were slaves. It didn't matter what they had seen or experienced as God's supernatural smart bombs annihilated the Egyptians into unconditional surrender, because in their minds, these Hebrews were mindless slaves. They were so oppressed in their thinking that they couldn't believe God's Word—even when they saw it manifested. The same is true for so many struggling individuals who are wandering in the desert of underachievement in our competitive world of today.

As an international ambassador at large of the Bahama Islands, I've encountered so many struggling people who could move up the rungs of life's ladder if not for this deadly underachiever disease. I have recognized this affliction in my studies of modern Russia's wilderness wanderings since they escaped their enslavement to Communism. While the hammer and sickle waved above their imposing iron curtain, the Politburo dictated when, where, how and why the citizens fulfilled their obligatory duties to the collective state. In return, the Soviet "citizens" were rationed basic housing and living needs. But today, years after their Communist deliverance, many are screaming to go back to "Egypt." Why? Nothing has been done to alter the nation's mind-set. The Russian pharaohs have evolved in their ideological mind-sets, and innovative thinking among the controlled citizenry is in tragic, short supply. Maybe they will break out of their doldrums yet. Seventy years of slavery is only a fifth of the time period ancient Israel spent as mindless puppets of the state. But for now they are wandering, much as the Hebrews did. So is much of the world's population who have experienced some form of prolonged oppression. This principle is true of spiritual oppression as well.

Stop and think about it—have you ever observed a coworker or business associate and said something like this? "You know, that man has been working in the same position for the last ten years. He's been given the same tools as I have, and he's still a functionary clerk in the durable goods warehouse." But the real question is, Has anyone been saying the same thing about you?

Information Doesn't Bring Transformation

The reason Mr. Jones or Mrs. Smith are still the way they are at the bottom of the corporate ladder is because information doesn't bring transformation; only conversion does. *It's not what you are that holds you back; it's what you think you are not.* So if you think you *are not* the caliber of person who can discipline your mind to obtain new knowledge, change where change is needed and excel to the top, you won't look at the bid sheets that are posted on corporate's bulletin board. But if you believe in yourself and are willing to take some risks, you can move up life's fickle ladder and keep a steady, improving ascent.

Now, let's look at this through the eyes of the Christian believer. Christians live and work in the real world. We don't live in a bubble. Take a look at your life. Has your work experience been glorifying God?

How successful has your journey been? Is a willingness to change the only distance that separates you from a thirty-five-day walk and forty years in the wilderness in your current life experience? Are you living in God's promised land of success and well-being today? Or are you wandering in the wilderness of mediocrity, with no vision for success?

How many times have you agreed in principle with something you heard or read, knowing it would improve your personal circumstances, but simply didn't do it? How many times have you said to yourself, "Yes, that's true. God is powerful, and He wants me out of Egypt...I know God has a better finance system than all of my credit-card debt...I know TV has become an idol in my life...I know this weight is getting out of hand...I know morning prayer and study need to get going...," but you didn't follow through? You may agree with the success principles of God recorded in the Bible, but until you share His supreme mind in the matter, His absolute conviction about them, no Bible truth or achievement plan will ever change your life.

The toughest part for Moses during that forty-year stretch of Promised Land highway must have been the reality of knowing that the only thing hampering Israel's forward progress was the *attitude in their minds. What you see and what you hear are small things compared to what you think.* It is the power of the mind that can move a young man or woman who was hired as a purchasing clerk into upper management by his or her fifth year of employment. It is also why another clerk may still be punching an hourly time clock in the same clerk's position ten years down the road. One is marking time and just trying to get by. The other is looking toward the next step through excellence and achievement. One believes and conceives; the other only hears.

The thinking process of the human mind changes only when the operator *conceives* and *believes* the input that flows into the eyes and ears. Conception must take place before there is any real change. Married couples realize that although the sexual act may occur many times, pregnancy will not occur until the woman conceives. And as any mother will tell you, when conception takes place, a change occurs. The woman's entire physiological makeup changes. Her hormones change. Her attitude changes. Her moods change. So does the way she views the future.

The same is true for employees who sit under the teachings and directions of senior executives. When the achievement truths their leaders are wanting to impart are conceived in the employee's heart, change occurs. That employee will excel in life, move up the corporate ladder and bring honor to his profession—once he conceives the truths of success.

It is also true for the church member who sits under the inerrant Word of God and finally conceives in his heart the truth of what he is hearing. A change will happen. The conceiving believer will go out and bring honor to God through his or her life. But the believer or employee who continually hears without conceiving will continue to sit with the same wilderness attitudes and problems he had before new opportunities presented themselves. Why? Because that is what that individual *willed*.

THE HUMAN WILL: THE MOST POWERFUL FORCE ON EARTH

THE HUMAN WILL is the most powerful force on earth. In the wilderness Israel proved that the Creator will not violate the human will or overpower the mind. You've proved this in your life, too. If you are living in a free society, today you are doing exactly what you want to do. *God can empower our minds, but we must empower our wills.*

The Christian life is a daily decision. Sometimes we think, *Wouldn't it be wonderful if every morning Jesus came into my bedroom, grabbed me by my collar and dragged me around all day to follow Him? Lord Jesus, manage my time, and make sure I stay in balance on my business appointments in relation to my spiritual appointments. Wouldn't it be nice, O God, if You, in an instant, would show me the wisdom of Your ways? Life would move on so smoothly, and I wouldn't have to take the time to read Your Word and pray every day.*

But life isn't like that. In fact, Jesus' thematic statement in Scripture was, "Whosoever will, let him come." The promised land is always before us, but we must come.

Bearing all of this in mind, I think I have discovered one place in the Bible where God seems to have failed. Now, I realize this is a very controversial statement because we have all been taught that God, in His supreme omnipotence, cannot fail. But when you look at that little bit of ground that mankind's Creator wanted to move His people across to possess their Promised Land, I think you would have to agree. God was unable to succeed expeditiously in the great exodus from Egypt. Why? Because He couldn't change the adult Hebrews' minds.

It was easier to deliver Israel from the power of Pharaoh than from the power of their own thinking. It was no problem to unleash God's mighty plagues and eventually drown Pharaoh's army. The problems began when the people made up their minds that neither God nor Moses had their best interests at heart.

This is particularly amazing to me because I have seen God perform some extraordinary miracles along the path of my life. Yet, I've never seen an ocean parted and never been allowed to walk through the piled-high waters. Neither have I seen supernatural clothing that doesn't wear out, supernatural fire by night to warm my campsite, a moving pillar of cloud by day to cool me from the desert heat. All of these visual wonders surrounding the Hebrew exodus were evident, but their presence didn't change the welfare state of mind held by these former Hebrew slaves.

And if the miraculous power of heaven couldn't change these former slaves' minds, neither will God's miracles change your thinking patterns. You may be awed at His demonstration and be moved in your trust and faith. But the only one who can change your mind is you. And God is looking for many minds to change in His church today so we can get out of the wilderness and fulfill His purpose in the promised land.

BORN TO MANAGE

WHEN YOU LOOK at the Bible through the eyes of God's purpose, you will see He is a God of "business." Because of my business training, I recognize this principle in the pages of Scripture for every eye to see. Yes, God is a God of purpose, potential, giving, principle, love and authority. But He is also a God of management. This means that if you're going to deal with God, you will have to start thinking management. If you're going to do business with God, you must reorganize your thinking and concepts. Why? Because everything God does is related to His management spirit. Leadership management was the reason for man's creation and the key to his fulfillment.

The first man was created to manage the planet. Adam was entrusted with earth's resources and instructed to manage and "fill" the earth. So let's get started thinking like God by first of all defining what management is.

Management is the efficient and effective use of

another's resources with the intent to give an account of your use of the resources to the one who entrusted those resources to you. The Bible calls this *stewardship*. If you stop to think about management this way, you will discover that you've been in business since you've known the Lord.

Everyone has had some resources entrusted to them. These resources can include children, abilities, creativity, finances, assets, your home and your yard, just to name a few. Therefore, everyone is a manager of something.

Now, speaking from a higher spiritual perspective, stewardship or management is the use of God's divinely endowed resources for the effective accomplishment of His earthly goals. The accountability in this model (as it was with Adam in the beginning) is man to God. If the believer is ever going to move out of the oppressive mind-set of slavery, this accountability model will have to be grasped.

MANAGING TO BE FREE

AS WE WILL learn in the pages that follow, living in Egypt was easy for the Israelites, because there *they* were the managed. The hard part came when God called them to manage, because most weren't up to the task. Freedom of choice and a free environment in which that choice can be exercised is the original purpose of God for every human being. So my number one responsibility to God is management—and so is yours. He gave that assignment to everyone, not just to your boss.

True freedom must be personally managed. But not everyone accepts this divinely endowed managerial responsibility. The people who learn to identify and manage their resources will always employ those who do not. It is the people who decide to take a chunk of the earth and manage it who become the earth's employers—both in and outside of the church world.

Think about the person for whom you work. There was a point in your employer's life when either he or she decided to stop being the managed, and a decision was made to start managing instead. It might have been a sewing machine, a print shop or a food store. Once your employer's business grew beyond his or her own ability and resources to manage, that person needed others to help them. So you were brought on board.

Now think about yourself. Where do you think you would be today if you had accepted God's personal stewardship calling twenty years ago and had managed His resources well? Would you be doing what you are doing today? Think about it.

One of God's greatest promises of kingdom living, found in Matthew 5:5, invites the meek to inherit the earth. Jesus wants His people to be so management efficient that their abilities and influence will be extended everywhere in the earth. God still wants His people to serve as earth's managers. Adam's charge of dominion hasn't changed. Jesus wants His church to be the earth's employers, not its employees. And we can be, once we learn to follow His management model of fruitful living.

Let's get started in responsible living by learning six unchangeable elements of management ability. They will work for you at home or on the job.

THE ELEMENTS OF MANAGEMENT

1. The authority

The freedom that waits on the other side of the wilderness must be prepared for and managed skillfully. The first element to be understood before arriving there is one's position under authority. Anyone in management must clearly understand who their boss is. And that person must know his or her own perimeters in the authority structure. What can or can't you do with the resources your overseeing authority has entrusted to you? What can or can't you do when engaging the business process?

2. The purpose of the authority

You must not only understand who has entrusted you with his resources, but also *why* his resources were entrusted to you. What was in your Creator's, or your employer's, mind when you were given those resources? When you understand this, then purpose will become the key to your judgment. It will rule your decision-making process.

If your boss entrusted you with a million dollars and directed you to earn a 20 percent return on it during the next year, you would know his purpose in releasing the funds to your care. He not only gave you the resources, but he also gave you the purpose for entrusting you with the resources. That information can guide and direct your judgment in making business investments. *Knowing the purpose of the authority placed in you is essential for success.*

3. The resources to be managed

In the process of becoming an effective manager, you

must also master your understanding of the resources or commodities for which you've been given authority. *Nothing in the world is worse than someone who doesn't understand what he possesses.* A man who sells his house, only to learn after it was sold that it sat upon a five-hundred-barrels-a-day oil well, didn't take the time to understand his resources.

It's the same with people. If you don't understand the value of your own talents and resources, people will try to buy you out cheaply. They will make you stay late and pay you bottom dollar. Your creativity will be taken advantage of as they keep you completely out of the company's profit margin. It works from the top down, too. If you are an honest department head, but you don't understand the skills of those working under you, you won't use them to their fullest potential. *You must understand both your own potential and the potential of those under your authority.*

4. The value of the resources

The fourth element of effective management is understanding the true value of every resource available to you. You can only manage effectively if you understand the full value of the resources you have. Jesus, the ultimate manager in history, understood the full value and use of birds and flowers, a value that few could understand. He said:

> Look at the birds of the air; they do not sow or reap or store away in barns, and yet your heavenly Father feeds them.... See how the lilies of the field grow. They do not labor or spin. Yet I tell

you that not even Solomon in all his splendor was
dressed like one of these.

—Matthew 6:26, 28

Jesus, the manifested Creator who manufactured
earth's birds and flowers, used them to teach His followers that one aspect of their intrinsic value was to
relax and trust God unwaveringly. How many humans
take the time to think about birds? Regularly we rush
through days, weeks and months without ever once
considering a flower. We walk by and ignore them.
Why? Because we don't recognize the value of what
they can teach us.

We should never allow our lives to become so hurried
or myopic that we ignore the value of the resources
around us—especially the people. People in general don't
value people enough. Jesus would pause in His teaching
of a large crowd just to bless children, heal a man's servant, raise a synagogue leader's daughter or talk with two
blind men whom the crowd was trying to shut up. (See
Matthew 8:5–19; 20:29–34; Mark 5:35–43; 10:13–16.)
Jesus understood the value of the resources around Him,
and because of His perception, He managed everything
effectively.

5. The responsibility that comes with the assignment

The fifth management element that must be understood is the responsibility that comes with the management assignment. You will be a good manager when you
know what you're accountable for and what is expected
of you. Look at the example of the Israelites. Israel could
have walked into Canaan in a month because of the
resources of God's promise and His power to perform it.

But they squandered their resources, and every one of the adults except Moses, Caleb and Joshua died in the sand.

Jesus taught an indicting parable regarding the common neglect in the management of our affairs. You will find it in Luke 16 under the heading of "The Unrighteous Steward."

The unrighteous steward in Christ's parable was unscrupulous and lazy. When his employer discovered his self-serving persona, he gave him two weeks (allegorically) to clear out his desk. The irresponsible manager responded by saying, "I know what I'll do so that, when I lose my job here, people will welcome me into their houses" (Luke 16:4). He then used his power of attorney to clear the books of some of his master's debtors by lowering their payments as personal favors to them. Although this man knew exactly what he had been held accountable to— even using it to his own advantage—he failed miserably at fulfilling his managerial obligations in his master's business affairs.

Jesus' indictment in verse 8 concludes the parable: "For the people of this world are more shrewd [wiser] in dealing with their own kind than are the people of the light."

The people of the world know how to make money, both scrupulously and illegally. This is a historic fact. But the indictment Jesus levels on the church in this parable is the fact that too many "children of light" neglect their responsibility in life's affairs. They allow the world to run over them because of their ignorance and irresponsibility in the business and social arenas. Jesus said His called-out followers were to be *in* the world, but not *of* it. That means His church should be doing it smarter, bigger and better than those who have not embraced God's kingdom principle. To do that, we must be disciplined and shrewdly trained in the organizational realities of our day.

6. The standards of expectation

The sixth leadership element in effective management is the necessity of understanding one's standards of expectation. Every assignment for management comes with an expectation. The person who makes you a department manager has a quality expectation of you. He expects certain things to happen in that department because of the resources entrusted.

It's the same in our relationship with God. God has given us stewardship of the planet, and He has certain standards He expects us to uphold. Unlike many business enterprises, the most important qualitative standard God expects from us is integrity. He wants everyone we encounter to know they have encountered the living God. And when we manage the resources He has entrusted to us in accordance with His standards of expectation, everyone will profit, not just a few.

MANAGEMENT COMES FIRST

BECAUSE MANAGEMENT BEGINS in our personal lives, each of these elements starts and ends at home—when no one is watching. If you don't have a management mentality, your behavior will produce the kind of mismanagement experience Israel encountered in the wilderness. Proverbs 23:7 tells us, "For as he thinks in his heart, so is he" (NKJV). The Israelites, like so many people of the world today, thought like slaves. And their thinking kept them out of their patriarch Abraham's Promised Land. Management is first of all a personal mental and spiritual decision. *Management begins in the mind.*

One of the points in Jesus' parable of the irresponsible manager had to do with submitted trust: "Whoever can be trusted with very little can also be trusted with much, and whoever is dishonest with very little will also be dishonest with much" (Luke 16:10). Our management ability determines how much of the *more* that God has for us has to be held back from us. God will give us as much of His *more* as we can be entrusted with.

Efficient management allows God to increase the *more*. I advise young people who are going to school or college to study management, even if their call is to Bible college. Even if they know what they want to study—biology, nursing, engineering or whatever—I still encourage them to take a management course, too. Why? Because the manager understands the responsibilities of freedom, and therefore he will end up employing the employees and leading the followers in society's affairs.

When I went to school to earn my master's degree, I decided I would not study theology; I took business administration instead. It was that business administration degree that made the difference in my ability to organize the relationships in my life, business and ministry. It gave me an expertise in recognizing the dynamics of management, leadership, communication and the value of things.

If you are involved in professional ministry, perhaps you relish your position in ministry but have relinquished the management of your home. You may like the title "Reverend" or "Doctor" attached to your name and may be completely absorbed with your ministry duties. But God isn't concerned with your title; He is concerned first with your management. Paul writes:

> He [the overseer] must manage his own family well and see that his children obey him with proper respect. (If anyone does not know how to manage his own family, how can he take care of God's church?)
>
> —1 TIMOTHY 3:4–5

So management is the key to life. If a pastor can't manage his own children, Paul says he is incapable of managing the children of God. Some Christian leaders are winning the world, but they are losing their own personal world. On a more administrative note, if a Christian leader can't manage his own bank account, how can God trust him with the $2 million bank account for an organization?

If in your current life experience, a willingness to change is the only distance that separates you from a thirty-five-day walk and forty years in the wilderness, how successful has your journey been? Are you living in God's promised land of success and well-being today? Or are you wandering in the wilderness of mediocrity, with no vision for success? Whatever you mismanage, you will lose.

I hope you have located yourself by now in relationship to your current condition in respect to God's management call. If you have been wandering, it is my hope the Lord will use the principles in this book to help you. God has a plan for the future side of your life (across

Jordan) that you will come to understand in the chapters that follow. A long walk to nowhere is not your destination. Jesus wants to make known to you the resources that are at your fingertips. So I ask you to go ahead and quickly review this chapter's principles and the six elements of management. Then, once you are satisfied with your working knowledge of them, I invite you to move on for a detailed study on irresponsibility. Once this most common trait of man has been done away with in a person's life, responsibility can set in.

Remember:

1. The authority
2. The purpose of the authority
3. The resources to be managed
4. The value of the resources
5. The responsibility that comes with the assignment
6. The standards of expectation

The most important person to change is yourself.

Principles of Freedom

Chapter 2
Falling Short of Freedom's Promise

1. You are made of the sum total of the choices and decisions you make every day.
2. It's not what you are that holds you back; it's what you think you are not.
3. What you see and what you hear are small things compared to what you think.
4. God can empower our minds, but we must empower our wills.
5. True freedom must be personally managed.
6. Knowing the purpose of the authority placed in you is essential for success.
7. Nothing in the world is worse than someone who doesn't understand what he possesses.
8. You must understand both your own potential and the potential of those under your authority.
9. Management begins in the mind.
10. Management is the key to life.

THREE

IRRESPONSIBILITY: FREEDOM'S DEADLIEST ENEMY

You are where you are because that is where you have subconsciously chosen to be.

NOTHING IN SOCIETY is more destructive than irresponsibility. The mismanagement of Adam has affected every generation of mankind since he partook of the forbidden fruit with his wife and tried to cover it up. Today, because of Adam's six-thousand-year-old transgression, the world in which we live is under the spell of this irresponsible spirit. Because of this, it is on a immovable collision course to its own self-destruction.

The reason we have such conflicts and debilitating experiences in the world today is because the world is filled with people infected by the irresponsible spirit.

THE SPIRIT OF IRRESPONSIBILITY

THE WORD *IRRESPONSIBILITY* means "not answerable to authority." Does that sound familiar? Many people in the world today don't want anyone telling them what to do. They want to do what they feel like doing, and they want to do it as long as they want to do it.

Irresponsibility also means "lacking a sense of account-ability or not liable or able to answer for consequences." Many people don't want to be accountable to anyone, including God's household of faith. When sin is con-fronted from the pulpit, the message is too often trans-ferred to the person sitting in the next pew. Our defensive line of thought is, *I pray for forgiveness, and He forgives me every time, so get off my back.* Few want to hear a pas-toral rebuke. Many Bible-toting, pew-warming Christians are living unclean lives; they don't want anyone to reprove or correct them. This is the spirit of irresponsibility.

The word *irresponsibility* also carries with it the meaning of "lacking conscience" or "unable or unwilling to respond to conscience." It is mankind's conscience that allows us to distinguish between right and wrong. When a lifestyle of irresponsibility is allowed to increase, the voice of conscience is progressively silenced. Some people are doing unbelievable things, yet they have no sense of guilt or remorse after they've finished. People are shooting each other. Husbands are beating their wives. Fathers sleep with their daughters, wake up, shower, eat breakfast and go off to work as if nothing has happened. Con-science has died throughout much of the world's society because we have inherited a spirit of irresponsibility.

To be *irresponsible* also means to be "fickle and change-able." Irresponsible people can be flighty, thoughtless, rash, undependable, unstable, loose, lax and immoral. They can have an unpredictable, unreliable and untrust-worthy character. And it's not just the "world's problem"; this spirit is also wild today in the Christian church.

THE BLAME GAME

IRRESPONSIBLE PEOPLE ARE experts at transferring blame for their own irresponsible actions. Remember Adam's defense: "God, the woman You gave me... remember, it was You who gave her to me... she gave me the fruit, and because You gave her to me, and she gave me the fruit... both of You... NOT ME... made me eat it! I'm innocent, God! Leave me alone!"

Everyone in our world today is an expert at blaming society for our own problems. People are caught in the mentality that takes no responsibility for their behaviors, decisions or the situations in which they find themselves. It all goes back to Adam's mismanagement in the Garden.

As we look at these definitions of irresponsibility, we see many of our communities in full disastrous bloom. *The entire world is suffering under the destructive influence of an irresponsible humanity.* We live in an irresponsible generation that believes the world owes it something. People refuse to take personal responsibility for their lives, decisions and actions. Can they turn to the church to help them find their responsible purpose in life? Yes, but the church must be established in her own responsible life.

THE ORIGIN OF IRRESPONSIBILITY

WHEN DID THIS spirit of irresponsibility enter our society? Again, the answer is simple. This destructive spirit was released in the Garden of Eden. In Genesis we find that the first man—who carried all men in his loins—violated his stewardship. Adam was given trust and responsibility for the entire earth. He had the responsibility to maintain the righteousness and holy standards of Creator God on this planet through obedience.

> And God blessed them, and God said unto them, Be fruitful, and multiply, and replenish the earth, and subdue it: and have dominion over the fish of the sea, and over the fowl of the air, and over every living thing that moveth upon the earth.
> —Genesis 1:28, kjv

The word *dominion* literally means "to lead, to manage, to control, to keep under and to be a steward over." God's command to Adam makes it plain that mankind was created to be managers over the earth. We were given responsibility to manage from the beginning. So we must look back at what happened in the Garden of Eden to understand where man's current plight began. Each of God's instructions to Adam fulfilled a specific purpose for mankind. Let's look at them.

Be Fruitful Through Work

When God gave Adam the Garden of Eden, the first thing He told Adam to do was to work.

> The Lord God took the man and put him in the Garden of Eden to work it and take care of it.
> —Genesis 2:15

God didn't tell Adam exactly what to do. He just told him to be productive. When God spoke to Adam, He was speaking to every generation of human descendants in his loins. When God said, "Adam, work," He was telling everyone to work. This indicates that work is a natural result of God's endowed responsibility.

Work is not a curse. It existed in the Garden when man was in perfect relationship with God. Therefore, if you don't like to work, you are resisting God's natural will for your life.

When Eve met Adam, he already had a job. So the first thing a man needs is not a wife, but a job. And a woman should never marry a man who doesn't want to work.

The word *fruitful* means "to produce results; profitable." To be fruitful, one must take out that which is hidden in a seed to let it flourish and grow. God's instruction to be fruitful wasn't limited to having children. God wanted Adam and Eve to be fruitful in everything. He placed "fruit" in the seed on the planet and commanded them to get the "fruit" out. The same is true for us. "And God blessed them, and God said unto them, Be fruitful" (Gen. 1:28, KJV).

This is why God never made a chair for Adam. Instead, He hid the chair in the tree. He never made a table for Adam; He put the table in the tree. He never made a car for Adam; He put the car in mountain ore and left the rest up to us. God simply gave Adam the raw materials, but it took Adam's ingenuity and productivity to be fruitful with the raw stuff.

Then God told Adam to name the animals (Gen. 2:19). He knew this would activate Adam's mental ability. Adam had a brain that had never been used, so God wanted Adam to try it out by naming all the animals. Can you imagine? There are millions of animals, and Adam's brain named every one of them. Before long, the first man began to realize he had potential that hadn't yet been tapped. *This is management—maximizing the resources under your care.*

This is why God always gives you something to do—so you can discover what you are *able* to do. Responsibility is the "ability to respond" to your God-given ability. So the only way to find out what you are *able* to do is to give yourself *something* to do.

MULTIPLY

TO BE FRUITFUL in filling the earth, there had to be human reproduction. So God put Adam, who was the source of all humans, to sleep.

> So the LORD God caused the man to fall into a deep sleep; and while he was sleeping, he took one of the man's ribs and closed up the place with flesh. Then the LORD God made a woman from the rib he had taken out of the man, and he brought her to the man.
> —GENESIS 2:21–22

Then God took Eve out of Adam's side, and He told them both to multiply and fill the whole earth.

Multiply means "to take what you produce and duplicate it so it can be disseminated." *Replenish* means "to be full of and accomplished." It also carries the meaning of "to distribute." To do this, Adam was to take what he did in the Garden and reproduce it in other places. That was God's plan.

God put Adam and Eve in Eden. The word *Eden* means "a location" or "spot." God took a spot on the earth and made it perfect. He also put His presence there, and everything in it was perfect. Then He told

Adam to duplicate his spot all over the planet until the whole world looked like it. If man had succeeded, he would have dominated the earth. This is what God wanted. God wanted man to replenish the earth by filling it with what was entrusted to his care. God wanted Adam to multiply the Garden so it would fill the earth.

HAVE DOMINION

GOD BLESSED OUR human parents and said, "Have dominion." He gave them responsibility to rule over the earth: "And have dominion over the fish of the sea, and over the fowl of the air, and over every living thing that moveth upon the earth" (Gen. 1:28, KJV).

This is the process of God, and it is no different for you or me. In God's management perspective, you don't dominate until you first become fruitful and productive. After you are fruitful, you have to reproduce or multiply what you produce. Then, after you multiply, you have to duplicate or distribute it until it fills your home, town and region—until it fills the whole earth. It is then that you have dominion.

The best way to keep people poor is to restrict their fruitfulness or productivity and to make sure they can't duplicate what they produce. The spirit of poverty causes people to be stripped of the power God gave them to multiply and to replenish the earth with their gifts. Greedy people will try to steal your idea to keep you from multiplying it. And when you are not being fruitful, productive and multiplying, you will be poor. Remember, when the Israelites were in Egypt, they produced only what the Egyptians said they could. So any creative gifts they might have had were oppressed.

MAN—THE FOUNDATION OF THE HOME

MAN IS THE foundation of the home because God began the human race with him alone. He was first, and he was created with every human descendent who was ever going to be born in his loins. This is why God didn't return to the soil when creating woman; woman was already made within Adam's being. God made one man from the soil and never went back to the soil.

Once Adam was formed, God instructed him about the tree. The "No Trespassing" sign was posted for his eyes alone. So get ready, men, because here comes a heavy burden of truth—God never told Eve about the tree. When the command about the tree was given, Eve hadn't even been fashioned from Adam yet. God instructed the male, which means God laid the foundation of the family in the male. It was the male who was responsible to keep his family away from that tree and to teach them about the commands of God.

If you want to destroy a building, do you break a window? No, you can break the window, but the building will stay intact. Can you knock a building into rubble by pulling a plank from the wall? No. Can you do it by tearing the roof off? No, that won't do it either. The only way you can effectively destroy a building is by wrecking its foundation, and the foundation of mankind's family is the first-made human—the male—man.

So if the foundation is faulty, the rest of the house will come tumbling down. Millions of women have suffered because Satan has always known that the male was the secret to the home. That's why the devil will try to keep the husband away from his wife. He will send the husband off or tempt him to abandon his wife and family. Why? Because as long as the male is not in place, the house is in despair. *The mismanagement of the male factor is the source of our family crisis.*

Over the years as I have counseled families I have learned that if you want to heal the family, you must reach the man. Women are often the first to make their family problems known. But the answer for healing lies in the man of the home, because he is the foundation of the family.

God gave the male all the instructions because He wanted the male to be the responsible manager and head of the home. *Head* does not mean "boss"; it means "the one who is responsible." When you are in charge of something it doesn't mean you created it; it means you are responsible for the management of it. If your home falls apart, as a male you are responsible for it. It is in this way that Adam was responsible for his family. But Adam stood there and watched as Eve fell prey to the tempter's snares. He should have stood up for his assignment and commanded the serpent to leave.

The man is responsible for sustaining whatever comes out of him. This is why the Bible never tells the wife to support or sustain the husband. It consistently instructs the husband to sustain the wife.

THE TRANSFER OF RESPONSIBILITY

ADAM DIDN'T SUSTAIN his wife; he irresponsibly neglected his position of leadership. Satan was then able to creep in and negotiate with Eve, thus successfully tempting her.

But it wasn't Eve that Satan was after. He was after the foundation of the human race—Adam. Wait, you say, Satan went after Eve. Oh, really? Let's look carefully at what the Bible says in Genesis 3:6.

> When the woman saw that the fruit of the tree was good for food and pleasing to the eye, and also desirable for gaining wisdom, she took some and ate it.

When Eve picked the fruit—nothing happened. When she ate the fruit—nothing happened. When she swallowed the fruit—nothing happened. So, when the woman sinned—nothing happened.

But then the Bible says she took the fruit and gave it to her husband, who was the foundation. And when Adam ate of it, death and all of mankind's mortal judgments entered in.

> She also gave some to her husband, who was with her, and he ate. *Then* the eyes of both of them were opened, and they realized they were naked; so they sewed fig leaves together and made coverings for themselves.
>
> —GENESIS 3:6–7, EMPHASIS ADDED

When Adam ate the fruit, *suddenly* everything fell apart. Death entered in. Their purity and holiness were gone.

> But the LORD God called to the man, "Where are you?" He answered, "I heard you in the garden, and I was afraid because I was naked; so I hid." And he said, "Who told you that you were naked? Have you eaten from the tree that I commanded you not to eat from?"
>
> —GENESIS 3:9–11

Please note, God did not ask for Eve. He asked for

Adam. God demanded accountability in His questioning of Adam, just as He questions us today when we fall down in life: "Did you do what I told you not to do, Adam?" "Did you do what I told you to do, Robert?" God makes a demand on the delegated responsibility He gives to His children. He wants to know if we have obeyed His directives or if we did our own thing. If we obey, there will be no need to run and hide.

Today, all men and women outside of Christ are hiding in fear from God. So are many Christians who are mismanaging their daily affairs. When most people break the law, they hide from authority as Adam did. Have you ever run a red light, then quickly glanced in the rearview mirror to see if a policeman saw you? When you broke the law—even if it was through oversight—what did you do? You checked for an authority. Fear came upon you. When you fail to keep the law, you condemn yourself. God never asked Adam if he was afraid. Adam volunteered the information before God questioned him on his obedience: "Did you eat from the tree, Adam? All this time I have been coming into the Garden you have never hidden from Me. You never ran. Yet all of a sudden you are afraid. Did you act irresponsibly?"

It was then, when Adam started blaming everyone but himself, that the spirit of irresponsibility and blame entered the human race. "The man said, 'The woman you put here with me—she gave me some fruit from the tree, and I ate it'" (Gen. 3:12).

Not only had Adam neglected to establish and uphold God's "No Trespassing" command, but after he watched Eve, Adam transferred the responsibility for his fruit-eating decision to the woman, who had offered

66

the fruit. "God, the woman You gave me...remember, it was You who gave her to me...she gave me the fruit. And because You gave her to me, and she gave me the fruit, both of you—NOT ME—are responsible for my decisions and actions!"

Now, if the woman had knocked him out, shoved the fruit in his mouth, pushed it down his esophagus into his stomach and made sure it got digested, then he could say she was responsible. But she didn't; it was Adam's choice.

I see people go to restaurants, eat all they can and then ask for a diet soda. I wonder, *Why drink a diet soda? You've already stuffed yourself.* It seems as if they're saying all that food jumped off the plate into their stomachs without their permission, so they're going to punish that food by giving it a diet soda.

Responsibility is a serious issue, but it's transferred too easily. "The woman you put here with me—she gave me some fruit from the tree, and I ate it" (v. 12). Adam even shifted the blame to God. In essence he was saying to God, "Why did You have to give her to me, God? Everything would have been OK if You had left things as they were. Now look what You've both done to me!" This pathetic transfer of responsibility has echoed throughout the human race for thousands of years since.

THE BLAME GAME

GOD TOLD ADAM to be the dominator of the earth. When Adam failed in that responsibility, his first reaction was to blame someone else. Ever since that day, man has transferred blame to someone else. All of us are professional blamers. No one wants to take responsibility for his actions, decisions, situations or circumstances. We blame others for our predicaments. Americans have ridiculous "Blame Game" television shows, on which the most abominable people appear and blame everyone but themselves for their miserable mistakes.

Today, more than ever, we are experts at blaming the past for our present. We are experts at blaming our parents for our habits. We are experts at blaming our preachers for our ignorance. Those of us who can't work algebra blame the educational system. When we had an opportunity to learn, we quit school or played hooky. Now we're algebra-ignorant, and we blame the teachers for our ignorance.

We love to blame sickness (instead of our poor judgment and eating habits) for our health problems. We eat poorly for thirty years, get high blood pressure and blame the devil because we don't feel well.

We blame our children for social problems. We say, "The youth do this, and the youth do that." But whose youth are they? If we as irresponsible adults produce irresponsible children, how can we blame our children for the problems in society? They are our children. So if our children are rotten fruit, we are the rotten trees from which they came.

We blame cigarettes and the tobacco companies for our cancer. I was shocked to hear a news story recently in which a woman sued a tobacco company because she acquired cancer through smoking their product. I can't understand that. She decided to smoke. She sucked that stuff into her lungs and got cancer all by herself. She chose to suck cancerettes when she was a teenager—she decided to do it! No company came to her door, tied her up and jammed a cigarette in her mouth!

Yet she cried, "The tobacco manufacturer made the

cigarette, and now look at me. It's all their fault!" How can someone who has the power of choice—the ability to refuse to smoke—remove the responsibility from herself and put it on the company that manufactured the product? Ask Adam! What an irresponsible lawsuit. And there are many other legal blame-game suits today in which the actions of the plaintiff are responsible for his or her own damage.

I've never seen a cigarette walk up to a guy and say, "Hey, buddy, smoke me." It's a decision that we make. Tobacco plants aren't the problem. The spirit of irresponsibility is what causes us to transfer our negative experience to the plant. If we could only get rid of that filthy plant, we say, then we could solve the nicotine problem. But the plant is not responsible for the problem. The human heart is the problem.

A drunk may blame the company, store or tavern that sold him the alcohol for his alcohol addiction. Yet if this same man never took a drink, he never would have become an alcoholic. It's amazing how alcohol jumps out of a bottle into a person's stomach. Some people spend twenty years guzzling the stuff, and finally end up in the doctor's office to get their liver fixed. Then they blame the doctor and sue him for malpractice when he fails.

How many men have been unfaithful and completely irresponsible with their families—then blame their wives' poor cooking for her grouchiness? Listen, brother, if she is grouchy, it is your fault because you have been a bad husband. Don't blame your wife for your irresponsibility.

Many men blame their wives for their waywardness. They say, "If you don't treat me right, I'll run around." And when they do, it's all *their wife's fault*. "She didn't do this right, or this enough..." And the reality of the situation is that the man allowed the spirit of irresponsibility to lure him away from his own responsibility, and he destroyed the foundation of his home.

Irresponsibility is freedom's deadliest enemy. People in every walk of life and from every ethnic background fall prey to it. Black people blame White people for their problems, just as White people blame Black people. The poor blame the rich. Citizens blame their government for unemployment. But can a government stop us from being productive if it allows the free choice of its people? So instead of waiting for the government to supply a job, why don't we use the brains between our ears? God gave us each five billion brain cells. It doesn't matter if you live in the ghetto of a Third World country. Even if the people in power are trying to restrict your productivity, one thing they can never do is rob you of your ability to think. When you submit your mind to God and put on your management cap, He will give you abilities, creative ideas and concepts that will astound your countrymen.

The government's job is not to provide employment. The Bible says government's function is to carry the sword of protection so the righteous can be productive. (See Romans 13:3–4; 1 Timothy 2:1–2.) God expects us to be in an environment where we can be productive without having to depend on the government to provide us with jobs.

The criminal blames society for his behavior. The homosexual blames his or her hormones for their perversion. Citizens blame their representatives for their nation's corruption. But if leaders are corrupt in a democratic republic, the people are at fault because they voted them into power. We produce after our kind.

We are experts at blaming our leaders. If your leader is blind, don't fall in his muddy hole and ask, "Why did you lead me here?" Don't blame the leader for the way you follow him; just stop following him.

How many people say they aren't going to be a Christian because they have seen too many hypocrites? So the sinner blames the hypocritical preacher for his own personal damnation. But blaming one's damnation to hell on a hypocritical preacher is foolish and irresponsible, because God never tells anyone to follow a hypocritical preacher. He tells us to follow Jesus. We must be responsible for following Him.

Let's Take Charge of Our Lives

A NEW DAY has dawned for the twenty-first-century believer and for every human to rise up to the task of taking our responsibility. So many people have become lazy because of the charismatic faith message that contends that if we say a certain prayer, God must "ante up"—regardless of whether we are managing our assignment properly or not. Divorce is running rampant, and many are being told that simple church attendance and tithing will make them rich. But God isn't making pew-sitting, faith-movement Christians rich because many have been mismanaging God's affairs in the home and on the job. God is not a game show host with a jackpot prize for religious contestants.

God is saying, "Irresponsibility is freedom's greatest enemy. Get back to responsibility. Men, take your place in the home. Manage My affairs and serve equally with your wife in My organizational structure. Organize your family according to My Word, and then increase your garden spot throughout the earth."

No matter what has happened in the past, we can take charge of our futures right now. Today is a new season of responsibility in which God is saying to each of us, whether you are poor, Black, White, rich, Indian—no matter who or where you are—"Stop blaming the system. Stop blaming the authorities. Stop blaming your parents. Stop blaming your pastor. Stop blaming your past. Get your act together, and become responsible managers, because this is God's will for you."

We can't change the past, but we can determine the quality of our future. We might not like the family into which we were born, but we sure can determine the kind of home in which we rear our children. The responsible choice is always ours, and when we choose to obey the ways of God, when we choose to nurture and obey His perfect spot of salvation in our hearts to replenish and fill the earth, He will back us up. The spirit of oppression produces the spirit of irresponsibility. Freedom demands responsibility.

Freedom—understanding its principles and the costs involved in irresponsibly mismanaging it—is what life is truly all about. In the next few chapters we are going back to the children of Israel's infamous days in the wilderness to examine the difference between deliverance and freedom from God's point of view. Let's begin by taking a closer look at how important it is to learn to manage the freedom that God wants each of us to experience in our own life.

Today, more than ever, we are experts at blaming the past for our present.

72

Chapter 3
Irresponsibility: Freedom's Deadliest Enemy

1. The entire world is suffering under the destructive influence of an irresponsible humanity.
2. Work is not a curse.
3. This is management—maximizing the resources under your care.
4. The best way to keep people poor is to restrict their fruitfulness or productivity and to make sure they can't duplicate what they produce.
5. The mismanagement of the male factor is the source of our family crisis.
6. Today, more than ever, we are experts at blaming the past for our present.
7. Irresponsibility is freedom's deadliest enemy.

FOUR

LEARNING TO MANAGE FREEDOM

What lies before us and what lies behind us are
tiny matters compared to what is within us.

I N THIS CHAPTER we are going to look at some important
principles of management and mismanagement that
will add some depth to the management elements covered in the second chapter. Nothing makes the owner
of a company angrier than a manager who thinks the
company and its resources belong to him personally. So
we will start in principle with the irresponsible realities
of mismanagement.

If you want to get fired very quickly on any job, go
ahead—I dare you to act as if you own it all. Take the
paper and paper clips home when you feel like it. Take
the computer home for your daughter's history report.
"Borrow" the fax machine for a few weeks. Just act as if
you own everything, and see what will happen. You'll be
fired so quickly you won't know how to manage the dis-
appointment.

The owner can take whatever he wants out of the office, whenever he wants, because he owns it all. But the manager can't. So if you mismanage the owner's resources, he will replace you. He has the right to come and get his resources anytime he wants, no matter where you put them. In essence, the manager is accountable to the owner. Stewards must be faithful to their proprietor.

PUNCHING THE TIME CLOCK FOR GOD

IN THE LARGER scheme of life, God owns His resources—the earth and everything in it. If we mismanage them, He will fire us and give them to someone else.

Jesus gave us an excellent example of this in His parable of the talents (Matt. 25:14–30). In this teaching, a master left some of his resources—in this case, money called "talents"—for his servants to invest while he was away. When he returned, he asked his servants to give an account for the resources he left in their care.

The servant who was given two talents doubled them to four. The servant who had five given to him doubled them to ten. But the servant who was given one mismanaged even that one. He buried it and didn't even earn interest on it. His master therefore commanded, "Take the talent from him and give it to the one who has the ten talents" (Matt. 25:28).

The master could deal with these men in the way that he did because they were investing *his* talents. When the third servant mismanaged the talent, the master took it from him.

Let's take a look at four principles of management that can be gleaned from this important teaching of Christ's.

THE FOUR PRINCIPLES OF MANAGEMENT

1. God created everything (stewardship is not ownership).

> In the beginning God created the heavens and the earth.
>
> —GENESIS 1:1

First of all, we must understand that God created and owns everything. He claims the right to it all, and He can therefore give it to—or take it from—whomever He wants, whenever He wants. Those of us who follow Him don't possess the right to claim anything we own as being ours. The minute we think we obtained it by our own ingenuity, God will make other arrangements with His investment. *God owns; we just manage.* Therefore, as long as we mismanage the resources entrusted to our care, God, who created and owns everything, will keep His resources from us.

2. God organized before He gave His best (order and organization are the foundations of management).

> And the earth was without form, and void; and darkness was upon the face of the deep. And the spirit of God moved upon the face of the waters.
>
> —GENESIS 1:2, KJV

In this second sentence of the Bible's revelation about earth and man's origin, the scripture says the earth was without form. That means it was out of formal order. The Hebrew word *tohuw*, translated "without form" in this verse, literally means "confusion." It speaks of the disorder of things. The word

76

implies that nothing was in formal order.

The Hebrew word for *void* is *bohuw*; it literally means "empty or void." It implies "chaos, confusion." So the earth was without a formal order or position. It was confused, disorganized and steeped in chaos.

A third word in this verse is *darkness*, which is translated from the Hebrew word *choshek*, and it means exactly what it says. But it also implies an absence of knowledge and revelation. Things were out of order; therefore, confusion reigned.

As you read Genesis 1 carefully, you will see that God created nothing between verses 3 through 26. Everything mentioned was already there. Verse 1 says, "In the beginning God created the heaven and the earth." As you read the text carefully, you will find that water initially covered all dry ground. You will also see that when dry ground was added as an earth component, the clouds, which were already present, had probably fallen from the firmament to rise up as a mist to water the ground. So although the heavens and earth had been created, they were disorderly and disorganized. Nothing yet was in its proper place.

Let's look at an example of something in a disordered, chaotic state like this. Let's suppose that you invite me to stay in your home for two weeks while you are on vacation. I accept, but I really don't like the way you have arranged your house. So I put the kitchen appliances in the bedroom and move your bedroom furniture into the bathroom. I change your living room into a bathroom and put your bathtub in the dining room. I change everything without taking anything out of the house. But my rearranging has taken everything out of formal order.

When you return home from vacation, you want to take a shower. So you go to the area that used to be your bathroom and find your bedroom furniture crowding the place. You look for the refrigerator, but it's not in the kitchen anymore. The result? Everything is present and in the house, but it is in the wrong place. This is the principle of disorder.

Disorder causes confusion—this is what *void* means. You don't know where everything is; you are in the dark about what is going on. This is how I see the Genesis account. In the beginning everything was present, but it was misplaced and out of order.

God saw the disorganization, but He had something special in mind. So He said, "I have this ultimate dream to create a being in My image and likeness who will rule and reign as a king over creation for Me. He will be My manager over the whole planet. *But I can't bring My best until I organize the rest.*"

So God turned the lights on to see the mess when He said, "Let there be light" (Gen. 1:4).

If your life is disorganized in the areas of finance, marriage, children or your job, don't keep stumbling in the dark. Stop and turn the lights on. When you do, you will see problems, and you won't like what you see. But you have to see your problems in the light before you can fix them.

God needed to shine the light on the confusion of creation so He could see what needed to be put into place. So He turned the light on and took a look. Then He pushed the clouds back up into the firmament and moved the water to produce dry ground. The water and land were there after creating it in Genesis 1:1; they were just in the wrong place. So He reorganized it. He raised up the ground and blew on it, and it dried up. Then He separated the salt water from the fresh water to make the lakes and the sea.

> And God said, "Let there be an expanse between the waters to separate water from water." So God made the expanse and separated the water under the expanse from the water above it. And it was so. God called the expanse "sky." And there was evening, and there was morning—the second day. And God said, "Let the water under the sky be gathered to one place, and let dry ground appear." And it was so. God called the dry ground "land," and the gathered waters he called "seas." And God saw that it was good.
>
> —Genesis 1:6–10

God also spoke to the soil and the water, because He knew what was buried in them. He said:

> Let the land produce vegetation.
>
> —Genesis 1:11

> Let the water teem with living creatures, and let birds fly above the earth across the expanse of the sky.
>
> —Genesis 1:20

> Let the land produce living creatures according to their kinds.
>
> —Genesis 1:24

In the ground God had created a wealth of trees, plants, fruit, birds, animals and all the great creation that mankind enjoys today. God just reorganized everything. And the Bible says that when it was all finished, "God saw that it was good" (Gen. 1:25).

God is a God of order. He loves organization and detests confusion (1 Cor. 14:33). So God withheld His best—the creation of man—until He was organized. He would not create man, who was the apex of His creation, until everything was in order. And when all was ready, God gave Adam an organized garden and said again, "It is good" (Gen. 1:31).

So here is the initial management message of Genesis for you: If you want God's best in your life, don't ask for the best—*organize for it.* Organization and order attract God's favor, blessings and resources.

3. God delegated management over the earth to man (man was created for the management of the earth).

Our third principle of management speaks of delegation. Man was created for the management of the earth. *Man was given rulership, not ownership, of the earth.* Genesis 1:26 says:

> Then God said, "Let us make man in our image, in our likeness, and let them rule over the fish of the sea and the birds of the air, over the livestock, over all the earth, and over all the creatures that move along the ground."

God granted man dominion and entrusted him with the resources He placed within the earth. God didn't give man the title deed to the earth, as some have taught, because He is the owner. Only He holds the title deed to everything we have right now. So God—who owns it—

can take it back whenever He sees mismanagement. His written will and testament states, "The earth is the Lord's, and the fulness thereof; the world, and they that dwell therein" (Ps. 24:1, KJV).

God owns your car. So if you don't want Him to take it away from you, clean it, service it and use it to bring people to the house of God. Use it to bless your children so you can say, "God, I'm using this thing, not just leaving it for display in my garage." Manage it.

Did you lose your house? If you did, it may not be the devil who took it. The bank repossessed your house because you didn't pay. Why didn't you pay? It wasn't the devil who had your money. Luke 16 says if you cannot manage another man's property, who will give you property of your own? So if He gave you your own house and you mismanaged it, He will put you back on another man's property to teach you management all over again. When you recognize setbacks in this light, you will see new opportunities instead of failure.

The New Testament writer Paul gives us a good teaching on delegation in the Book of Galatians. In Galatians 3:26 he tells us, "You are all sons of God through faith in Christ Jesus." Then he continues in Galatians 4:1–2, "As long as the heir is a child, he is no different from a slave, although he owns the whole estate. He is subject to guardians and trustees until the time set by his father."

The message of these verses tells us that children of inheritance are treated like employees in regard to their inheritance when they are children. Why? Children don't manage things well. If you give a child a jar of peanut butter, it will soon be all over his face, head and eyes. He doesn't manage the peanut butter; it manages him as he puts it everywhere it shouldn't go. Give your child a beautiful diamond ring, and he will chew on it for a while. Then he will spit it out or throw it through the window where the dog will pick it up and run off with it. A child is a mismanager. So, even though Jesus Christ is Lord, and we are His sons through the re-creation of our spirits by faith, God doesn't trust any of us with His estate until we are mature. *God will give you what you can manage, not what you ask for.*

What is the key to His giving you more ownership in the estate? Let's look at what parents do. They don't release authority until children are capable of managing the authority.

The earth is the Lord's, and the Lord is your Father. And since you are His son, you are heir to the gold, silver, trees—everything. But we can't just walk around waiting for God to dump stuff in our laps. *We must learn how to manage in order to receive from God.*

One of the most mismanaged areas in the lives of believers who need God's light today is the area of personal finances. Many Christians borrow money continually and never stop to realize that they don't own themselves anymore. The next time someone comes to you and asks you for money, ask that person to whom else he owes money. Why? Because people never ask the person they already owe for more money. They create bigger problems by going to new people with the same old problem. They perpetuate their own darkness and stumble around, never stopping to turn the light on.

If you are deeply in debt, don't get nervous about the thousands you owe. Stop. Take a good look at your situation. Don't be afraid to see that you owe money to half of the folks in your family, church or community. Realize why you avoid those you owe and slip through the back door. Be honest with those you owe. Turn the light on and confess your obligations. This will start the training process through which God can mature you. Integrity is the key to everything we do.

First, hold yourself accountable to God, who delegates all. Then, enlighten yourself to see how much you owe. Take a piece of paper and add up all the amounts you owe to people. Then, because debt doesn't go away by avoiding it or hoping your debtors don't call, hold yourself accountable to call each debtor and check the numbers. Let them know you're sincere about paying back every cent.

Have you noticed that you can't pray phone bills out of existence or cast light bills out in Jesus' name? Being filled with the Holy Spirit doesn't cancel any debt. Unless there's a miracle, you still owe the money.

Prosperity is not dependent on the resources God gives you, but on your delegated management of what you are given. So never pray for things you are not willing to manage. If you don't feel ready or qualified to manage something, don't waste your prayer, because God will withhold from you what you will mismanage.

When a child inherits money, it is placed in the management of a guardian or trustee until he or she is mature enough to handle it wisely. The same is true of your inheritance on earth. *God gave you rulership, not ownership, so He can always take back what you mismanage.* The problem is, when He withholds or removes resources from us, He usually gives it to people

83

who are not too far from where we live. And many times those people may not necessarily be committed to His kingdom, although they are good managers.

We have this funny idea in the church that everything is for the righteous. Proverbs 13:22 does say that "a sinner's wealth is stored up for the righteous," but let me tell you, if you mismanage, God will give it to the unrighteous. *Oh, Dr. Munroe, what are you saying?* I can hear you thinking. But listen: God allowed the devil to have the earth. We can see that in Luke 4 when Satan offered Jesus the kingdoms of the world with their wealth if Jesus would bow down and worship him. "For it has been given to me," the devil said (Luke 4:5). Jesus didn't bow, of course, but neither did He dispute the devil's claim that the world and its kingdoms had been given over to him.

The devil will hold on to whatever is yours until God trains you to manage it. As you will see in coming chapters, you must raise the cows for the milk and scoop the honey out of stinging beehives to get your milk and honey in the land that God has promised you. And until you can take them from him, the devil will hold on to your goods.

Using this Promised Land allegory, the wicked of this earth are guardians holding on to the wealth of the righteous until the righteous are ready and qualified to manage it. They have been placed in these positions by God, but what they have doesn't belong to them—it belongs to us. Remember the scripture: "The wealth of the sinner is laid up for the just" (Prov. 13:22, KJV). But the question is: How did the wicked get the wealth? And, does God know they have it?

Some people are bitter toward the rich. They hate "those wealthy people." When they pass by their two-story houses up the street, they get jealous thinking about their crowded, little house with its small kitchen. Stop being jealous. Those people learned how to manage and earned your dream house. You've been trying to fast and pray it out of their hands, but it hasn't moved because God doesn't move resources as a result of prayer. He moves resources as a result of efficient management. When you prove faithful over a little, He will make you ruler over more (Matt. 25:23). *Management attracts resources.*

4. God gave clear assignment and instructions (you must understand the assignment and instructions).

The fourth management principle we want to deal with has to do with understanding the will and objectives of the one for whom you are managing. God clearly told Adam his assignment: He was to work, cultivate and protect (Gen. 1:28). Then He gave Adam the instructions: He was not to eat of one particular tree (Gen. 2:17). Adam had no question about his assignment or instructions. He was directed to manage the earth, and he was to obey God implicitly.

The forbidden tree wasn't a setup to trick man. With His instruction to avoid the one tree, God established a fulcrum where man's conscience and will power could be activated and come into obedience. Adam was not a robot but a creature of will with the power of choice. He was a free agent. The power of "will" is activated by the power of choice. Therefore, the tree was forbidden in order to *activate* Adam's will power—not to *destroy* it.

God was Adam's Creator, Father and Boss. It is impossible for you to be a proper manager if you don't

85

obey the boss. You can't manage the company any way you feel like doing it. You have to stay in touch with the boss's vision and the company's vision. If you manage Kentucky Fried Chicken, you can't decide you want to make hamburgers. You can't manage without obedience to the authority in the company.

Every time you mismanage, your incompetent reputation will follow you. If you get fired from a job because you've mismanaged the company's resources and you apply for another job, the first question they usually ask is who your former employer was. So don't think that you can mismanage and start over fresh. God will always take you back to where you stumbled until you learn to manage right.

I was recently talking to a young man who had mismanaged his business and was in financial straits. I told him to accept whatever job he was offered, no matter how humbling it was. He used to be in business for himself. But now, because of poor judgment, he needed to go back to the bottom so he could regain his credibility and work himself back up to the top. I told him to start over again so his employer could see consistency, faithfulness and management to rebuild trust. Then I told him that when God saw his new diligence, He would entrust more to him once again. The young man was teachable, so I know he will be fine. Some I have counseled to humble themselves again at the bottom haven't been as teachable as he was. They want to start where they blew it, but restoration doesn't work that way.

Every Christian believer has a clear responsibility to manage God's resources well. People who keep jumping from problem to problem will never be given much. God knows right where those people are. Every time they show up, He is there waiting for them. When they ask for something, God tells them no. Why? Because God protects His resources from mismanagers—including mismanagers who are full of the Spirit, speak in tongues and know the Bible.

Sin Is a Product of Mismanagement

If GOD's FUNDAMENTAL purpose for man is management, man's fundamental problem is mismanagement. And that's true. Why are three-fourths of the world's people living in poverty? Why are you having such a hard time living on your meager salary and struggling to keep a job? If you are a business owner, why is your business having such a hard time? Why don't people have the money to buy your product? The answer: mismanagement.

When you look at the Scriptures with your management hat on, you will see that man's number one problem is not sin. It's mismanagement. Sin is the result of Adam's mismanagement. Let me show you what I mean.

The introduction of sin to humanity was actually a mismanagement problem. God's first man was given a job to oversee the Garden, and he literally sold out the company to an illegal entity, the devil. Adam made the worst of deals. And because of Adam's gross mismanagement, sin, with all of its destruction, was unleashed within the earth. God's command to Adam was: "Have dominion over the earth and everything in it." The word *dominion* means "to govern, rule, control, cultivate and order." In essence, God gave Adam the management contract for earth. Another word used for management is *stewardship*.

If Adam would have managed his affairs properly,

mankind as we know it would have remained as he once was. But Adam mismanaged. And since the loss of Adam's management commitment in the beginning, all of mankind has followed in his footsteps as incompetent mismanagers. We've mismanaged the environment so that many lakes and rivers are contaminated. Earth's air is full of contaminants. Our water teems with pollutants. We've poisoned earth's fish with lead and other toxins, and on occasion we murder our entrusted livestock through "accidental" poisoning. We've mismanaged the whole thing to the point that our actions are killing ourselves. Greed has overshadowed our common sense. Fallen man prefers to line his own pockets with his greed-gotten gain instead of ensuring that the environment is safe. God has been trying to reinstill His management perspective into the human race since we lost it in Genesis 3.

Mankind was created to be managers, but now we're experts at mismanaging. This is why our Third World countries today have such problems. Many Third World leaders are responsible for countries that are rich in natural resources, but the people stay poor due to mismanagement. *When people mismanage, God protects His resources from them.*

Every time you spend a dollar without being aware of the value of that dollar, God will take another dollar out of your control. I believe God is frugal, and that every time you spend money on something for which you cannot justify its reasonable value before God, you give Him the right to take that money from you. I know this because of my dealings with Him.

And I will tell you, God will bless you financially if you are in the center of His will, managing wisely the resources

He provides you. People are amazed at the multimillion-dollar facility that He has allowed us to build in Nassau of the Bahamas. If I were to misuse the provision designated for building, television, outreach or inreach on a whim, He would find someone else to bless. He would take our ministry dollars and give them to someone else. This is why people who mismanage always get poorer and poorer.

Many governments, and the nations they oversee, are poor because of mismanagement. Haiti is the oldest republic in the Caribbean and was the first country to gain independence, yet it is the still the poorest country in the region.

Trinidad has oil, Jamaica has bauxite and Guyana and Nigeria are rich with gold. Yet every one of these countries is borrowing money and is a victim of the International Monetary Fund (IMF). Why? Because of greed, misplaced priorities, mismanagement, distorted ambitions and personal agendas. *Poverty is ultimately a product of mismanagement.*

God created everything, and He will not have it mismanaged. He will keep it from people if they don't oversee their resources with intelligent oversight.

Some people have so much money they'll never spend it in their lifetime. I heard of a baseball player who received a contract for $91 million over five years to play baseball—you know, hitting a little ball made of leather with a piece of wood. I couldn't cheer that announcement because I think about the millions of poor people who need that $91 million. And I'm sure God isn't excited about that.

No wonder God allows the earth to be cursed. No wonder we have so much tension, crime and difficulty.

It's because the earth and its resources are mismanaged.

The poor of this earth deserve a better life. *But God will only give people what they won't waste.* People who have much get more because they manage well, and the poor who are poor because of laziness and mismanagement will probably always be jealous of them.

These mismanagement principles are eternal. If you don't learn them, the results and the consequences of violating them will be evident. You will always be poor and depressed. You will always live as a beggar below your privilege.

Now that we have defined the problem, let's look in more detail at some mismanagement principles from Genesis. Any management-minded person will want to avoid these principles. Remember, the first syllable of management is "man," because it is his destiny and design.

FIVE PRINCIPLES OF MISMANAGEMENT

1. Misuse of resources produces mismanagement.

> When the woman saw that the fruit of the tree was good for food and pleasing to the eye, and also desirable for gaining wisdom, she took some and ate it.
>
> —GENESIS 3:6

First of all, let us notice that in the Garden, Adam and Eve abused the fruit on God's one forbidden tree. They did with it what it was not made to do—they ate it. So, they mismanaged it. *Whenever you misuse resources, you have become a mismanager.*

If you dump junk food and harmful substances into your body, which was entrusted to you by God as His holy temple, that's mismanagement. And when you mis-manage what God gave you, you will lose it. Eventually your health will begin to fade, and on the day you planned to celebrate your wedding anniversary, your spouse may be attending a funeral instead—yours. Why? *Misuse leads to mismanagement.*

2. Misappropriation of resources brings disqualification and guilt.

Have you ever prayed for a need, perhaps for some money, and you received it? Maybe you received an unexpected check in the mail from something you did five years ago. Or perhaps you told the Lord you needed an extra $200 to pay for a specific thing, and the money came in. But when the money came, the specific thing you needed it for lost its importance. Suddenly all those other things you had been wanting seemed more important, and you misappropriated the money. This kind of misap-propriation will disqualify you for management. When-ever you misappropriate material, whether it's money, property or people, you become disqualified to manage that resource. God will no longer trust you. He will put a hold on your spiritual account until you pass Manage-ment 101. The principle is: "Whatever you mismanage, you will lose."

The same is true with borrowing. Have you ever bor-rowed money for something specific, then spent the money on something else like shopping, groceries or taking a trip? If this happens, the next time you ask for something, God will remember what you did with the last thing He supplied you. In this case, your misappro-priation will put you out there on your own with you and you alone to pay back the loan.

When Adam and Eve disobeyed God's command and misappropriated His property and resources, they were disqualified. They were kicked out of their own Daddy's company! And if Daddy puts you out, you're in real trouble.

Do you think it's possible that effective management can be more important than sonship to God? I don't know about you, but the simple idea of it all spins my head. Adam was made in God's image and in His likeness. He was God's "son," yet God put him out of the Garden of Eden. Why? Because he mismanaged God's property. It's frightening to think about, but being a child of God doesn't qualify you for God's blessings. Yes, you are brought into the family, but it is your ability to manage the things of God that qualifies you for His blessings. If every Christian was guaranteed success simply because of conversion, we would see the results. Everyone would be full and prosperous. But we don't see that, and I believe that management is the key.

Don't worry, God will forgive any of your mismanagement episodes, but He won't trust you again automatically. If you've sinned by mismanaging your time with the wrong people, or if you've damaged your body and mind with corrupt materials, come to God and ask for His forgiveness, and He will forgive you. But He will want to see you grow up in His wisdom before He trusts you with anything again. If you sinned with His money by spending it on new clothes instead of the rent, God will forgive you. But he won't give you more money until you learn to pay the rent.

People who are disciplined in this area attract God to them. God increases their resources everywhere they go. Why? He lets them have things because they don't misappropriate them. He trusts them. Jesus stressed the importance of management as a prerequisite for trust in His statement: "The meek shall inherit the earth." The word *meek* denotes self-control and self-discipline. The result is rulership over earth's real estate.

3. The responsibility of management cannot be transferred.

This principle points to the fact that because you are breathing, it is you who are responsible for the management of your life. You cannot abdicate your responsibility and hold someone else accountable for your daily affairs. Whenever anyone tries to shift his life over to another's care, God literally takes what he had from him.

Let me show you what I mean. Adam tried to transfer his management responsibility to Eve. We do the same thing. We may watch a television program and buy into those advertisements that hype new sneakers, clothes, perfume or cars. People buy into them because they appeal to their lusts and covetousness. As a result, we buy something we don't need. When someone asks us why we bought that item, pointing out its expense, we respond, "I saw it advertised on TV, and it just seemed right."

When anyone engages in this kind of behavior, that person is transferring the managerial responsibility of his life and resources to some hype-driven marketing company. When called to accountability, the person attempts to avoid taking responsibility for his irresponsibility. "This woman," he says, "jumped out of my TV, grabbed me by my suit, dragged me down to the store, slapped me a couple of times to make sure I still wanted the item, MADE me buy it, then took me back home and said,

'Now be satisfied.'" But when he is not satisfied, and he is sorry he made the purchase, then it wasn't his fault—the lady in the tight jeans on TV made him buy it!

If you're not careful, the poor (or those who are called poor) can cause you to mismanage God's money irresponsibly. I met a young man who was begging for money at a stop sign one day. "Oh, you're a pastor," he said. "I know you are a good man of God, so you will surely give me something." He was about twenty-nine years old, but he looked more like thirty-nine—or even forty-nine. I even knew the guy. We went to school together. "Come on, preacher," he continued, "you are a man of God, I know you can't say no."

So I looked at him and asked, "How old are you?"

"You know me, man. We went to school together," he replied.

"You're right," I answered. "So if I were to give you any money, I would be making you poorer, and I would be abusing God's resources."

The man looked confounded and asked what in the world I was talking about. So I continued, "Hop in my car. When we get back to my office, I want you to clean my car. And if you do a really good job, I'll pay you for your work."

"What are you talking about?" he complained in astonishment. "I didn't ask you for a job! I want some money!"

"No," I answered. "In the name of Jesus, NO." He was so shocked he couldn't even curse.

I looked into his glazed eyes and said, "You don't need money; you need work."

The man didn't want a job; he wanted to manipulate me into a handout, so he hurried off. If I had given that man some of the resources God had entrusted to me, he would have certainly run off and used it to finance his irresponsible lifestyle. I would have been held accountable for contributing to his condition.

We have to be careful that we aren't manipulated by other people through our emotions, because that could lead to the misappropriation of our money. We might be giving to a drug addict's illegal drug fund and to various other causes of people whom God calls wicked. What a waste; what a shame. That young man had a brain, talent, energy, gifts and strength—I knew it because I knew him— but he was a mismanager. *If you support and finance a mismanager, you become complicit in his foolishness and can become part of his mismanagement sin.*

Nothing in the world attracts me like people who are trying hard to make it. When people are really trying hard, it makes me want to dig down inside my pocket and bless them. The great King Solomon says in his proverb: "Lazy hands make a man poor, but diligent hands bring wrath" (Prov. 10:4).

I am compassionate toward the genuinely poor. I make myself available to help them get out of their situation. But when someone is lazy and trying to get something for nothing, it really turns me off.

God has called us to work, so I try to make it available to those who need it. Look at what Paul said in reference to church widows in 1 Timothy 5 (Paul took a tougher stance than I do, believe it or not): "Give proper recognition to those widows who are really in need. . . . As for younger widows, do not put them on such a list" (vv. 3, 11).

Paul tells Timothy to take care of the older widows

95

who have no one to help them. But he tells the younger widows to stop being busybodies, get remarried, keep house and get to work. (See verses 13–15.)

"Help me, I lost my job," a young widow could have told Paul.

"Well, come and let me introduce you to Orpheus who may know someone who could give you another one," Paul answers. "And if that doesn't work out, you can clean my house."

"I ain't no maid!" she shouts while stomping off.

"Then you don't want any blessing," the apostle says while shaking his head.

This may sound particularly rough. But you can't transfer responsibility for management to other people, even if your circumstance is as unfortunate as a poor young widow's. You, and you alone, are responsible for what you are supposed to manage. God will give you the opportunity, but you must receive. You were created to manage effectively your intellect, body, mind, creativity, time and relationships.

4. Whatever you mismanage, you will lose.

This mismanagement principle embodies the saddest words in Scripture: "So the LORD God banished him from the Garden of Eden" (Gen. 3:23).

When Adam mismanaged his job assignment in the Garden, he not only lost his job—he also lost his home. He was kicked out of the Garden. To whom did God give the Garden? He gave it to man. Who took the Garden from man? God did. Who put him out? God did. Let's get that straight again. The devil didn't put Adam out of the Garden—God did.

In fact, God is so serious about management that He may even assign angels to guard His property from you because of your mismanagement. That's what He did with Adam, so why wouldn't He do it with you?

> After he drove the man out, he placed on the east side of the Garden of Eden cherubim and a flaming sword flashing back and forth to guard the way to the tree of life.
>
> —GENESIS 3:24

God doesn't waste His property. He also apparently values it so highly that He will use angelic intervention to protect it from abuse. Angels holding flaming swords could very possibly be guarding the way back into squandered ministries and businesses at this very moment because of the foolishness shown by those who mismanaged them.

God intelligently uses His resources to their fullest and expects the same from man. What did Jesus instruct His disciples to do after He fed the five thousand? "Gather the pieces that are left over. Let nothing be wasted" (John 6:12).

Jesus said, "Pick up every crumb. Nothing here is to go to waste." Why? Because God doesn't sponsor mismanagement. Jesus possessed a management mentality. He detested waste. If you want to attract much, manage the little.

5. Mismanagement may be "personal," but it is never "private."

This fifth mismanagement principle tells us that when you mismanage, you are not the only one affected. Adam mismanaged just one man—himself. He

97

did it personally, but it certainly wasn't a private issue because his sin has affected every man and woman on earth. Because of Adam, Moses tells us, "[God] does not leave the guilty unpunished; he punishes the children and their children for the sin of the fathers to the third and fourth generation" (Exod. 34:7). And the apostle Paul writes, "Through one man sin entered the world, and death through sin" (Rom. 5:12, NKJV). There is no such thing as a private sin. All men today are fallen because of one man's mismanagement.

There is a very revealing law in economics that says that you can tell mismanagement is taking place in a nation when the nation's people have to pay more taxes. When there is corruption in high places, or when there's mismanagement anywhere in government, it is the people who have to pay for it. This demonstrates clearly that people pay publicly for personal and private mismanagement.

Let's bring this down to where you live. Say you bring home a stapler from your job. *They won't miss it,* you rationalize. *They're a big company. They have two hundred staplers.* But when there are ten thieves on staff (just like you), and they decide to steal "privately" (just like you), now ten staplers are gone. But no one of the ten knows the other nine are doing it.

OK, so you think you got away with the theft of the stapler. Now you take home some copier paper, just a hundred plain sheets. No problem, they have ten thousand sheets. But a hundred other employees are also doing it. All of a sudden the company sees that their profits are being used up by the unauthorized disappearance of materials. So next year the boss says, "Last year we lost money because we had to replace a hundred staplers, a hundred thousand sheets of paper and about fifteen thousand staples. So this year we are going to have to lay off three people. You, you and you. In addition, there will be no bonuses this year. And by the way, there will be no raises. We are also going to freeze all salary increases for the next three years until our company gets out of the red and back into the black."

Now your "private" acts have put three people in the unemployment line. The company has streamlined its investments and isn't buying materials from the community because it's smaller now. The businesses who sold them paper aren't making as much, so they, in turn, must lay people off. Your thefts have contributed to putting all those people out on the street.

Let's push this up to an even higher extreme. Because these people who were laid off due to curtailed business can't find jobs, they break into your house. Now there is a crime problem, thanks to your theft of the stapler and copy paper. The government has to hire more police, and they have to tax everybody more to pay the salaries. When the police apprehend these former clerks and cashiers (now turned thieves), there isn't any room in the prisons. So more tax money is needed to build another prison. Where do you think all the money is going to come from? From you! Who else? When the new prison is built, they need new guards, new administration, new food and new cooks for the prisoners. So there's more taxation to support this prison.

Do you get the picture? The cycle of mismanagement that began with the theft of one stapler never ends. In this same manner, the corrupt mismanagement of one—or twenty—government official works itself down to enslave people's lives. The Third World is reeling from such "private" sins. *Mismanagement may be personal, but it is never private, because it affects everyone.*

You may mismanage your body personally by sleeping with someone in "secret." No problem. You had a good time, and no one knows. Right? Wrong! Because one day, all of a sudden you have a sore on your nose. The doctor says you have a little infection, so they do some blood tests and find out that you have the HIV virus. "Oh, you're married?" the doctor asks. "Bring your wife tomorrow." So you do, and because your wife is pregnant, now you have a wife and child with HIV. Your personal sin is not a private issue.

"But it was so private, God!" No, it wasn't. And because of your irresponsibility, generations to come will be contaminated by your private mismanagement.

Think about the resources God has given you. Are they still in your possession, but out of their proper place? Turn the lights on in your marriage, children, job, house and car, and start to think organizationally. Make this confession right now: "Heavenly Father, I am sobered by this reality, so please, help me to grow in my management calling. I promise to manage better from this day forward." Let's move forward now in the Bible's redemptive history to visit with and learn from the children of Israel. Their pilgrimage from oppression to freedom has many lessons for each of us. It was their struggle with the management issue that caused them to forfeit the Promised Land.

Principles of Management

1. God created everything (stewardship is not ownership).
2. God organized before He gave His best (order and organization are the foundations of management).
3. God delegated management over the earth to man (man was created for the management of the earth).
4. God gave clear assignment and instructions (you must understand the assignment and instructions).

Principles of Mismanagement

1. Misuse of resources produces mismanagement.
2. Misappropriation of resources brings disqualification and guilt.
3. The responsibility of management cannot be transferred.
4. Whatever you mismanage, you will lose.
5. Mismanagement may be "personal," but it is never "private."

God is more interested in your character than your comfort.

PRINCIPLES OF FREEDOM

CHAPTER 4
LEARNING TO MANAGE FREEDOM

1. God owns; we just manage.
2. Man was given rulership, not ownership, of the earth.
3. God will give you what you can manage, not what you ask for.
4. We must learn how to manage in order to receive from God.
5. Prosperity is not dependent on the resources God gives you, but on your delegated management of what you are given.
6. God gave you rulership, not ownership, so He can always take back what you mismanage.
7. The devil will hold on to whatever is yours until God trains you to manage it.
8. Management attracts resources.
9. Mankind was created to be managers, but now we're experts at mismanaging.
10. When people mismanage, God protects His resources from them.
11. Poverty is ultimately a product of mismanagement.
12. God will only give people what they won't waste.
13. Whenever you misuse resources, you have become a mismanager.
14. Misuse leads to mismanagement.
15. If you support and finance a mismanager, you become complicit in his foolishness and can become part of his mismanagement sin.
16. God doesn't waste His property.
17. Mismanagement may be personal, but it is never private, because it affects everyone.

FIVE

THE SPIRIT OF OPPRESSION

You cannot hold a man down without staying down with him.

—*BOOKER T. WASHINGTON*

"WAKE UP! WAKE up! You slaves, wake up! It's 4:30 and time to wake up!"

"You there! You have been privileged to help your filthy friends raise Pharaoh's pylon today, so get your filthy carcass up to the overseer now, or I will help you with the whip!"

It must have been something like that to live in Egypt when Israel was held in bondage. The only way the slave drivers got people to work was with a whip. Oxen weren't given a shower or time to "brush their teeth," so neither were Pharaoh's slaves—who were no more than simple beasts of burden to Pharaoh and his evil overseers. Can you imagine what it must have been like to be awakened by a whip?

Once they were aroused from their sleep, the Israelites were driven into the field with whips, where

103

they bent over all day to make bricks out of mud and straw. They hated it. The work imposed on them just added to their hatred of their enforced bondage. This is the reason why the oppressed have a negative attitude toward work even after they are delivered. It reminds them of their oppression. People who have been oppressed or have lived under the spirit of slavery develop a dislike for work.

Every time Israel took a rest, they had to be whipped to get them back on the job. The slave drivers wanted work, not rest. The children of Israel became over-whelmingly tired as the sun baked their skin and sweat poured down their faces and aching backs. Still the whips cracked over them constantly to keep them on the task. "Keep working! Keep working, you miserable slaves, or I'll give you something you can really feel miserable about!"

Two Names, One Enemy— Oppression and Irresponsibility

WHEN PEOPLE ARE oppressed—in any generation or any people—they develop a spirit of irresponsibility and a hatred for work. Many individuals today are carrying the baggage of their former oppression. Work isn't viewed as an opportunity to glorify God and receive His promotion; it is viewed as an obligation—merely a way to pay the bills.

After a while, the Israelites believed work was equated with pain. It was accompanied always by pressure, distress and the whip—which caused such pain. When they were finally delivered, they equated their deliverance to the absence of work and greatly rejoiced

(Exod. 15:1, 20). In their "retirement," they thought, *We made it! Retirement time! Fishing boats, hammocks, golf courses, tennis courts—no more work*! And that's just how so many think today. Historically, formerly oppressed people always dream of going to a type of heaven where they will finally be free. Some even dream about getting a million dollars so they can quit work. If you think that way and do stumble across the money, God will probably take the million from you to send you back to work, because work is not a curse. It's the first thing God gave man to do (Gen. 2:15).

Don't hate work. Love work. Develop a passion for the thing that God gave you to do. Do it the way Jesus did it. "'My food,' said Jesus, 'is to do the will of him who sent me and to finish his work'" (John 4:34).

When your work becomes as important as three meals a day, you are becoming a responsible person. When they have to pull you away from your work to eat, you are coming close to the spirit of responsibility. But if you can't wait for lunch time, you have the wrong spirit. If you start work at 9 A.M., and you can't wait for the coffee break, you have the wrong spirit. If you stretch out your break and read the papers until it's lunch time, you have a slave-minded spirit.

People who hate work can't handle time. They become irritated and depressed when they have time on their hands, because time demands the responsibility of deciding how to spend it. They love it when people drive them and tell them what to do, because they have the spirit of the slave. And because nothing a slave does is for his own good, people who have been oppressed for years have difficulty with productivity. Most Third World and developing nations are suffering from this today.

Do you know how the prosperity of a country is measured? It is measured by the Gross National Product (GNP). The wealth of a country isn't measured by how much money they have in the national treasury, but by how much the people are producing. When the majority of your people have lived their lives under the whip of poverty and oppression, productivity suffers and the country stays poor. GNP simply means the collective productivity of the nation's citizenry.

OPPRESSION PRODUCES LAZINESS

ANOTHER EFFECT OF oppression is laziness. People who have been oppressed suffer from a spirit of laziness because they equate work with suffering and pain. If one has been forced to do a particular task all his life, as Israel was, and then is released from that obligation, that person will stop doing everything that was once forced upon him to do. The Israelites only did what they did twenty-four hours a day because they were forced to do it. Yet many of the things they were forced to do were good. It is possible for constructive, necessary things like housecleaning, yard work—even personal hygiene—if forced upon a person in servitude, to become unwelcome, disdained kinds of work. Even when that person is no longer forced to do those things, they may remain activities to avoid.

This kind of laziness is a product of the oppression itself. People don't want to be lazy. But they do become lazy from being the managed instead of the manager. They lose their energy and enthusiasm because of oppressive restraints put upon them that keep them from being self-productive. *Oppression actually conditions people to be unproductive, and laziness becomes a lifestyle.* Lack of self-motivation and initiative prevail.

In Egypt, the children of Israel didn't have to find their own food. They didn't have to pay for their own houses. They didn't have to find their own water. They didn't have to find their own clothes. They didn't have to find anything because Pharaoh provided everything to keep them on the job. The oppressor provides everything for the oppressed in order to protect and maintain his investment.

Then when Moses led them out of Egypt, they had only been in the wilderness a few weeks when they started murmuring and became angry. What was their complaint? They "had no food!" They "had no water!" So they complained to Moses:

> If we only had died by the LORD's hand in Egypt! There we sat around pots of meat and ate all the food we wanted, but you have brought us out into this desert to starve this entire assembly to death.
> —EXODUS 16:3

The Israelites equated existing for a little while without food as a premeditated attempt to kill them. Why? *Oppressed people are quick to accuse when they are no longer receiving the provisions of their servitude.* They can't handle tough times. They can't handle a little lapse in the system of welfare. In this manner, oppression makes people lazy.

FEAR

PEOPLE WHO ARE oppressed are also full of fear. They are

fearful because everything they see is painful to them. Everything that happens to them is viewed as a power play to force them into doing something they don't want to do. So they avoid responsibility and live in fear.

Fear also comes from not knowing what your oppressors are going to do to you. Every time one of Pharaoh's soldiers showed up, the Israelites began to shake. Every time they saw a whip, they started trembling. And that spirit of fear didn't leave just because they left Egypt. They stayed and wandered forty years in that little patch of desert I viewed during my Israel-to-Cairo flight, when it could have been crossed in one short month. Fear kept them bound to that ground outside of Canaan, just as it keeps millions bound to their own oppression and poverty today.

Oppressed people are afraid of everything, even their own people. They cringe at the thought of anyone gaining power over them, especially those who were once oppressed with them.

Bearing all of this in mind, oppressed people view their employers as taskmasters bearing the whip. So they are intimidated by what they *perceive* as the oppressor when the boss walks into their office. As soon as he or she shows up, they feel unimportant. What's wrong? They're still intimidated. Fear lives in them even in freedom.

OPPRESSION AND DELIVERANCE—THE MIND AT WAR

THIS SAME THING happens spiritually after people have been delivered from sin. They see someone they used to hang out with or take drugs with—and fear comes in because they feel that they might be weak and go with them. They sometimes resist new church leaders in church and hide out from volunteer work. This is why Paul told Timothy, "God has not given us a spirit of fear, but of power and of love and of a sound mind" (2 Tim. 1:7, NKJV). God has not given the believer a spirit of fear, but we must believe it.

Once we submit to the redemptive work of God in Christ Jesus, we need to admit that we used to be bound. But deliverance is not freedom, so we must embark on the adventure of learning to walk in the kind of responsibility that will actually set us free. As we will examine in coming chapters, the wilderness is a place of preparation for freedom, but too many die there without ever being free.

This spirit of oppression in the church environment is deadly because it stops people from doing what God created them to do. They fear the thought of stepping out into the new territory—the very territory that will bring them freedom.

Unless revelation changes the mind of a new believer, when that person is delivered from a lifestyle of sin, he or she will continue to do exactly what sin had conditioned him or her to do. That's the power of oppression. Even a delivered and released man is afraid to be productive because he is afraid of going beyond the barriers that bound him during his oppression.

Low Self-Esteem

Low self-esteem is another effect of living under oppression. If someone has been oppressed, he begins to believe that *down* is where he belongs. If he is invited *up*, he will give a list of reasons why *up* is not the place for him.

I've observed this feeling of low self-esteem in many people in my own country, the Bahamas, and in many other nations. People can be oppressed by law through some oppressive regime or by a parent. Then, when they gain a measure of deliverance, they still have to deal with a spirit of low self-esteem. If you invite them to a nice place, they say, "That's all right, you didn't have to do that." If you buy them something nice, they will tell you that you didn't have to do it. They will try to hand it back. And if you can get them to receive it, they will apologize for receiving it.

If an oppressed person goes to a palace and is served caviar at the table, he can't eat it. He's too busy describing the tablecloth and looking at the gold forks. He doesn't believe he can eat with such nice things. He doesn't believe he deserves the best.

The free, confident man may use his good bone china every day. But the oppressed man who has never had anything won't—the good bone china stays in the china closet. He has difficulty believing that he has any value, so valuable things appear in his own eyes as too valuable for him. I dare some of you reading this to take out those expensive dishes you've been saving for company and start using them. Why? You deserve to use them.

I told my wife a few years ago that our kids are going to use everything. Why? I don't want them to look at certain dishes as if those dishes were too good for their use. That's the thinking of an oppressed person. The king doesn't put his golden chalice in a cupboard and drink out of plastic cups. He figures, "I'm a king. I deserve a king's cup."

This may seem a minor issue, but you may not be completely free until you can use your wedding dishes again. You may not be free until you can put salad in that expensive bowl and tell your children to eat with the silver forks—every day. Go ahead, wear out your bone china. It isn't reserved for some prince in France. Use it. You're the prince.

Do you have rooms in your house into which no one goes? For whom are you reserving them? Walk on that carpet; sit in that chair. Wear that thing out, and God will provide another one. Don't go into debt and cause your family pressure, but if the Lord blesses you, go ahead and appreciate the blessing. Enjoy the benefits.

The oppressor will never allow those he oppresses to be equal with him because this minimizes his superiority, which he used in his oppression of others. He has to reduce those he preys upon to less than who they really are so he can justify his oppression. Therefore, oppressed people are so low in their estimation of themselves that they don't believe they deserve anything good. Low self-esteem plagues their lives because the oppressor gave them an estimation of themselves that made them look insignificant and small.

POOR SELF-CONCEPT

THE NEXT DEADLY fruit of oppression is poor self-concept. Some people are told all their lives that they are nothing and that they will never amount to anything. After a while they believe it. Once they believe it, they are in trouble, because it takes an entire generation to remove the spirit of a poor self-concept and low self-worth, except by a divine interruption.

It is important to remember that every human is created equally in God's image and likeness, and all are therefore inherently the same in value.

No one can make you a human. You were born a

human. Therefore, no one has the right to assign value to you—or to devalue you. Human value is not dependent upon what others think about us. It is inherent in who we are because of our creation by God.

The value of the gold ring on my finger isn't determined by what you think about it. You may say the ring is stupid or worthless, but it's still gold. You may say it's plastic, but it's still gold. You may say it's retarded, depressed and ugly, but it's still gold. What you think about it has nothing to do with what it is.

Civil rights can legally grant a ring to sit on my finger while the value of the thing is still in dispute. So don't confuse civil rights with human rights. In America, Martin Luther King, Jr. was only a deliverer, but the freedom to which he opened the legal right must still be possessed. My own country has enjoyed emancipation from the British crown since 1973, and we have only recently been growing into the measure of the kind of national freedom that allows us to work and think truly free. At first we had parades and danced, just like Miriam and the Israelites did on the other side of the Red Sea. But when the music died down, we saw how much we had to learn before actually becoming free. We needed education and training to prepare for positions of authority. I was privileged to spend some time as assistant to the Secretary of Education in my country's government, so I was able to be involved in many of our new learning programs.

The principle issue is not civil rights, even though this is important. The true issue is human rights. *It is human rights, not civil rights, that set people free.* I could give you permission to vote but still look at you as inferior and inhuman.

Your value is not determined by what people think about you. It is determined by where you came from—and you came out of God. You were made in His image.

SELFISHNESS

OPPRESSION ALSO PRODUCES the spirit of selfishness. If an oppressed person who never had anything suddenly gets something, he hangs on to it with his life. This is how oppression promotes selfishness, and this is why oppressed people can be very dangerous. If they ever get a position of power, everyone is in trouble. Oppression breeds greed.

When those who are oppressed in their minds get something they never had before, they protect it. They build a wall around it with barbed wire and hire look-outs. If you come into their little world, they will attempt to destroy you. Greed breeds more greed. "Things" begin to represent a false prestige and power, and those who threaten their accumulation are viewed as pests worthy of elimination. If you don't believe me, look at world history—countries have gone to war over treasure and land. The spirit of selfishness also manifests itself in the mind-set (attitude) of immediate gratification. This is the desire to demand instant pleasure and satisfaction. Oppression makes the status symbol of the oppressors to be the object of pursuit for the oppressed at the expense of development, personal growth and maturity.

LACK OF CREATIVITY

ONE OF THE most defeating aspects of human oppression is the dull thinking that comes with it. The spirit of irresponsibility that comes from oppression brings a lack of creativity. If you have been told what to do all your life, you stop using your mind.

Oppressors don't want those they oppress to think for themselves. So they try to keep them ignorant, and they do everything in their power to keep them from getting a good education. The oppressor doesn't want the oppressed to expand their minds and get knowledge. It is ignorance that gives and maintains the power of oppression, so they use it as a tool.

When things get tough, our brains should kick in creatively. It is then that we figure out how we are going to put food on the table. But if we never have to figure things out, our brains shut down. It is in those tough times that free thinkers will sew those dresses, cook that rice or sell those cakes. We'll do something. God will make us industrious when He pulls Pharaoh's support out from under us.

God wants us to be inventive. Once we are delivered, He will give us a revelation of how creative we can be. I mean, God may turn our electricity off just so we can remember how to make a fire and how to cook in an open pit.

For most, as soon as we turn the gas stove on and it doesn't work, we get irritated and transfer this responsibility to someone else. Try thinking instead. Stop and think for a minute when a problem arises. Cut some wood and kindling, break out the matches and start your fire. Use your brain. Be responsible.

If you lose your house, don't sit down and cry. You didn't have one before you got the one you lost. Rent another one. Start over again. Do something. Don't just throw the towel in and say, "That's it." Too many people wander aimlessly after their deliverance. God gave us fantastic brains, so be creative. In deliverance, God will allow many challenges so that He can once again activate our creativity, initiative and intellectual potential. Oppression destroys creativity and breeds dependency.

God gave you the ability to deal effectively with everything that comes against you. This is why Paul writes:

> God is faithful; he will not let you be tempted beyond what you can bear. But when you are tempted, he will also provide a way out so that you can stand up under it.
>
> —1 Corinthians 10:13

The apostle Paul probably grew up in one of the most modern and well-provided-for homes of his day. He was a full Roman citizen and a full Jew. He had doctorates in law and theology from the top academic school of his day and a thriving career in Hebrew government.

Then one day God pulled the rug out from under him. Suddenly he had no home and no job, and he had lost all his old well-to-do friends. But that was fine with him, because he was also finally free. "I know what it is to be in need, and I know what it is to have plenty," he wrote to one of the many churches he started. "I have learned the secret of being content in any and every situation, whether well fed or hungry, whether living in plenty or in want. I can do everything through him who gives me strength" (Phil. 4:12–13).

Paul was an oppressor who found out through his deliverance how oppressed he really was. So after his deliverance, he had to change his way of thinking. If he could do it, so can you. Suddenly his salary was dependent upon God and God alone. He was highly educated, but the keepers of the temple had no use for a washed-up Christian convert such as he. So one day he had a thought: *tents.* Paul remembered that he knew how to make tents. And that is what he did to support his new life.

God won't allow you to be tempted beyond what you can handle. And even if you do make a mistake, God knew you were going to make it before you made it. But He also knew that He put in you the ability to work your way out of that mistake. Paul certainly made his share, but he grew from them all—and so can you.

Some people who have been delivered but who still battle oppression must be shown how to do everything. Their creativity level is so low that they can't take an assignment and put it into action through their own resourcefulness.

An oppressed person with no creativity may acquire land, but he can't think how to use it. So a man comes and buys the land from him for $50,000. *Oh, what a lot of money,* the seller thinks. But the man from Idaho grows potatoes, and the land becomes worth $15 million. The oppressed man wasn't creative enough to see beyond the dirt's $50,000 worth, so he takes the $50,000 and lets the management-minded thinker make an annual mint.

The spirit of irresponsibility always says, "This can't be done; this has never been done. No one ever did it like this; we can't do it like this. This can't happen here." But management's spirit of responsibility knows all things are possible. *The spirit of responsibility knows there is always a way to accomplish everything.*

Sometimes we ask God to fix something, but God wants us to use our brains to maximize ourselves. "Listen!" He says. "I've given you a brain with ten billion cells. I've given you imagination. I've given you knowledge. I've given you wisdom. I've given you insight. I've given you foresight. I've given you hindsight. I've given you sight! So why are you still coming to Me, wanting to know how to fix it? You fix it! Put your free-thinking management cap on. Think!"

The Holy Spirit will work with a human spirit as a member of His new creation management team. That's why He is called the *paracletus*. A *paraclete* is "one who comes alongside to help." He doesn't move in to take over your business, and He doesn't muscle in to take over your home or your dreams. He comes to *help* you make things happen and to manage them, because He is the *Helper*.

Are you waiting on God? Maybe His Holy Spirit is waiting on you. He's a helper; He's an assistant. But He can't assist a man who isn't doing anything! Remember Christ's wisdom in recognizing resources and the resource-trading servant in the parable of the talents? Birds and flowers teach us God's love and trusting faith. His parable teaches us that we have unknown resources within us that God wants us to recognize and develop. So put on your management thinking cap. What can you do today to improve your situation? The Holy Spirit will help you once you decide to get up and move.

DISTRUST

WHEN PEOPLE HAVE been oppressed, they learn to distrust their brothers because of the spirit of survival. *The spirit of oppression and slavery also produces jealousy, distrust, suspicion and hate.* When you are oppressed, all you want to do is make it through the day. You'll use anybody to get ahead and to survive life's miseries with more comfort. This is why people who have been oppressed usually fight each other. They don't trust one another, especially when one of them starts to move ahead. They are fearful of a power play, so they band together to pull any achiever back down.

LACK OF INITIATIVE

BECAUSE OF ALL the restrictive and inhibiting effects of oppression, the nonthinking tendencies of this condition naturally take the initiative from a person. It is that initiative that would drive him to do things for himself. People who have been in bondage for a long time have almost no personal drive left. They are told when to get up, when to go to this spot, when to chip these rocks, when to rest, when to eat and drink and when to stop. Then they are told when they can go to the bathroom, when they can go to bed and when to get up. "Get up! Time to make more of Pharaoh's bricks!"

When the oppressed obtain their deliverance, they still want someone to tell them what to do. When God says, "Work out your own salvation" (Phil. 2:12, NKJV), they panic and groan, "Jesus, I thought You were going to work it out for me!"

If an individual still suffering from the spirit of oppression doesn't receive an opportunity to develop his or her potential after deliverance, that person will become a parasite who looks to others to take responsibility for his or her life. Jesus leads and guides us and tells us how to do things. But He gives us the responsibility of doing our part. So if we don't pray, read the Word, stay in fellowship, follow God's direction, read good books, listen to good tapes and build ourselves up, we will drift.

Oppression's instilled selfishness, fear, laziness, poor self-concept and hatred for work have ruined many lives. But the good news is that irresponsibility can be turned around. God wants to improve the skills of the responsible and give new abilities to those who have none. He wants to make managers out of mismanagers, and responsible adults out of all of His children.

We need to act on our faith. Once we come to Christ, we must resist the oppressive thoughts of our past and decide to rid ourselves of any former laziness. We must decide to get up earlier to read those books we keep putting off or to go jogging. We must decide to get that mind and that body back in shape. The choice is always ours to get up earlier, pray a little longer and strengthen our relationship with God. When we do, the Holy Spirit will help us. But the act of choosing is always up to us.

Now, let's move on into chapter six to look at some lessons the Hebrew children teach us through their wilderness exploits.

The greater the obstacle overcome, the greater the personal development.

PRINCIPLES OF FREEDOM

CHAPTER 5
THE SPIRIT OF OPPRESSION

1. When your work becomes as important as three meals a day, you are becoming a responsible person.
2. Oppression actually conditions people to be unproductive, and laziness becomes a lifestyle.
3. Oppressed people are quick to accuse when they are no longer receiving the provisions of their servitude.
4. Oppressed people are afraid of everything, even their own people.
5. It is human rights, not civil rights, that set people free.
6. The spirit of responsibility knows there is always a way to accomplish everything.
7. The spirit of oppression and slavery also produces jealousy, distrust, suspicion and hate.

SIX

WILDERNESS PEOPLE

We see things not as they are, but as we are.

ISRAEL'S LIFE AT the end of a whip ended with their deliverance, but the whip-beaten thoughts from their four centuries of oppression followed them into the Red Sea.

I can almost imagine what Israel's physical forty-year crossing of Sinai must have looked like from God's point of view. The terrain was etched in my mind the day I looked down from my airliner seat while flying the short distance between Israel and Cairo.

The hot desert sun that my wife, Ruth, and I felt while traveling that ground on foot was the sun Moses felt burning on his back.

The dust and barren hills we saw were viewed and even hiked on by the massive Hebrew horde.

The Books of Exodus, Leviticus and Numbers fill in my imagination's blanks with the actual account of what transpired thirty-four hundred years ago when the elder slaves of Moses' wilderness expedition failed in their attempt at freedom and died in Sinai's dust.

But there were also those who did make it to the other side of the Jordan. In this chapter we will look at the lessons we can learn from both groups—the parents and the younger generation of Israelites. The truths about the parents are important because they warn us against the pitfalls of oppressive and rebellious thinking. But the truths about the children are just as important—they can help us break out of our bondages.

The parallels between individuals and the developing process of nations and the Hebrew's Egyptian exodus are amazing in their similarities. Let's do some wandering now along Israel's wilderness roads.

RESPONSIBLE LIVING BEGINS WITH A PROMISE

THE FIRST LESSON Israel teaches us is that God's call to responsible living always begins with a promise. Before Israel moved into Egypt under the direction and care of Jacob's son Joseph, the family's patriarch, Abraham, was given a promise:

> I will make you into a great nation and I will bless you...all peoples on earth will be blessed through you.
>
> —GENESIS 12:2–3

There was a famine in the land of Israel, so Joseph, who had been sold into Egyptian slavery and was eventually promoted to be Pharaoh's prime minister because of his management skills, invited his family to eat and dwell in the safety of Egypt. After Pharaoh and Joseph died, a new Egyptian king who didn't know about Joseph enslaved the Hebrews. But although the Israelites had now become enslaved in Egypt, God had not forgotten His promise to Abraham.

The way in which God handled the children of Israel is the way He still handles all individuals and nations. So let's look at two principles about the promises of God.

GOD GIVES A PROMISE BEFORE HE FULFILLS IT TO CREATE A VISION

THIS FIRST PRINCIPLE makes sense, doesn't it? You don't promise something that has already been given. So the first important point we need to see in this chapter is that God always begins with the end result. He is always working toward the goal of your successful freedom, but He needs you to capture and believe the vision for it. God gives you a vision of freedom while you are in slavery.

The process of Israel's deliverance began with Abraham's promise, which established the Hebrew nation. But when it was time for their deliverance from Egyptian bondage, God renewed the promise—this time to Moses as he stood barefoot before Sinai's burning bush: "I have come down to rescue them from the hand of the Egyptians and to bring them up out of that land into a good and spacious land, a land flowing with milk and honey" (Exod. 3:8).

Now, this was some kind of promise. God described to Moses the land He had promised Abraham as Abraham never heard it. Everything would be beautiful, perfect, prosperous, flowing with milk and honey, spacious and good. A vision is a promise of a preferred future, and God has promised the same to all mankind and to every nation.

God has promised every man, woman and child on earth a hope for the future and a heavenly experience. Every human was created to fulfill a promise. You are the product of a promise. But now note the second principle of God's manward promise:

GOD ALWAYS GIVES THE PROMISE WHILE YOU ARE STILL IN SLAVERY

GOD TELLS YOU His good news while you are in the middle of a bad experience. He tells you about freedom while you are in the midst of slavery. When He tells you about the top, you are lying at the bottom. Why? Because promises are always made for future fulfillment, and they are meant to bring hope. That's what hope is all about. *A promise gives birth to vision. Promises give birth to faith.*

God promised Abraham that he would become a great nation. But when the time came to fulfill that promise, the Israelites were struggling at the bottom of life's experience in Egyptian slavery. So in fulfillment of His promise, God raised up Moses, who accepted the management call to set the Hebrews free. *A divine promise is more powerful than your predicament.* God's promise was to take the people from slavery to freedom. He promised them milk and honey while they were eating garlic and onions. However, what He did not tell them was the process necessary to get them to freedom.

THE THREE PHASES OF FREEDOM ALONG RESPONSIBILITY'S ROAD

MEN, WOMEN AND nations today must progress through the same three phases of deliverance in the process of freedom as Moses moved through to deliver the Israelites.

The road to responsibility runs through the highways of the world, down into the Red Sea, out into the wilderness and then through the Jordan River into the promised land. So the first phase of deliverance is bondage—or Egypt. The second phase is the wilderness. And the third phase is the crossing of the Jordan River into the promised land. Every nation and individual, small or great, young or old, must pass through these three phases on their way to true freedom. And as I pointed out in the previous chapters, if you can't overcome the realities of your past, a wilderness experience is all you can expect. True freedom is always a matter of the mind and heart.

THE EGYPT PHASE

THE EGYPT PHASE is the time of oppression and bondage. Israel was in bondage in Egypt for over four hundred years. They were depressed, oppressed, suppressed and (some) probably *possessed* as slaves for ten generations. Look at their history as recorded in Exodus 1:

> So they put slave masters over them to oppress them with forced labor, and they built Pithom and Rameses as store cities for Pharaoh. But the more they were oppressed, the more they multiplied and spread; so the Egyptians came to dread the Israelites and worked them ruthlessly. They made their lives bitter with hard labor in brick and mortar and with all kinds of work in the fields; in all their hard labor the Egyptians used them ruthlessly.
>
> —EXODUS 1:11–14

125

The daily burden and mistreatment of this enslaved people moved them to cry out for freedom daily. "The Israelites groaned in their slavery and cried out, and their cry for help because of their slavery went up to God" (Exod. 2:23). God heard their cries according to verses 24–25:

> God heard their groaning and he remembered his covenant with Abraham, with Isaac and with Jacob. So God looked on the Israelites and was concerned about them.

God raised up a deliverer from the very palace halls of Egypt. Pulled from the bulrushes of the Nile by Pharaoh's daughter to be raised as her own, Moses would be Israel's deliverer. Called from the shepherd fields of Midian at the age of eighty, God would use him supernaturally as a forerunner of Jesus to show all men how futile it is to attempt salvation in a natural sense. Moses, before he became a fugitive, attempted to deliver his people through his own strategy—and killed an Egyptian.

When Moses or his brother and ministry partner, Aaron, raised his simple shepherd staff, God turned it into a miraculous tool of deliverance. Great plagues were unleashed on Egypt to display God's divinity. As they left Egypt and entered the wilderness journey, the Red Sea opened, manna came down from heaven, pillars of fire and cloud kept them warm and cool respectively while guiding their way, water gushed out of rocks and clothes remained fresh and clean every step of the Hebrews' way. This was a shadow and type of salvation in Christ today, because mankind is saved by God's miraculous grace, not by religious works. Deliverance is always miraculous.

When Jesus walked among men, He proved the reality of God's love and divinity through the many miracles God worked through Him. Jesus walked on water, healed the sick, commanded fish in the lake to fill fishing nets, fed thousands miraculously, calmed storms with His word and raised the dead. Then He bled, died and rose again to save us without our permission. Mankind can't do a thing to save himself. Jesus did it all. All we have to do is agree with Him, and He saves us. We can't die for ourselves, and there is no good work that can "earn" salvation. Jesus did everything He needed to do to deliver us from sin (Egypt).

The miraculous signs that God performed when Moses lifted his staff brought down miraculous plagues that weakened Pharaoh and delivered Israel from their mud pens to the Sinai. There was nothing natural about their deliverance—it was miraculous. And this is exactly how God sets people free from their Egypt phase today—miraculously.

Today God sends the Holy Spirit to confirm His reality through miraculous signs and wonders, and He reaches into our hearts to make us new creations in our inner man. Paul writes:

> Therefore, if anyone is in Christ, he is a new creation; the old has gone, the new has come!
> —2 Corinthians 5:17

Only God can do this. It's all a miracle. Then He leads us into the next phase of deliverance on the road to freedom through the miraculous parting of our own Red Sea.

THE RED SEA PHASE

THE SECOND PHASE on the road to freedom begins with the Red Sea deliverance phase, which always leads to the wilderness. Remember, God didn't take the Israelites directly from Egypt to Canaan. He took them to the wilderness to get Egypt out of them first.

It was in Egypt that God worked His delivering miracles. When the plagues of bloody water, frogs, gnats, boils, hailstones mixed with fire, locust and darkness fell upon the Egyptians, Israel was kept safe as the plagues hit all around them. But it was in Sinai that God worked His provisional miracles. The Sinai wilderness experience is characterized by God's miraculous provision.

So many teach Israel's wilderness experience as nothing more than an agonizing time of failed dreams and failure. And for the elder slave-minded Hebrews, for the most part that was true. But the wilderness was also where God comforted and provided miraculously for the Hebrews in abundance. It is during our early years of faith in the wilderness that we live on God's miraculous manna. He does everything during that period without any contribution on our part. The same is true of nations. When God gives birth to a new nation, He provides a period of grace and wealth so they can learn and prepare for the responsibility of freedom.

First, God takes us from Egypt through His miracle power that parts the Red Sea.

> Then Moses stretched out his hand over the sea, and all that night the LORD drove the sea back with a strong east wind and turned it into dry land. The waters were divided, and the Israelites

went through the sea on dry ground, with a wall
of water on their right and on their left.

—Exodus 14:21–22

Then once we are delivered from the oppressor and
enter the wilderness, we receive God's miraculous
bread from heaven as our daily food. In deliverance,
God miraculously provides and meets our needs.

Then the Lord said to Moses, "I will rain down
bread from heaven for you."

—Exodus 16:4

If we are honest in our seeking and find ourselves in
need of God's miracle power, He will bring water forth
from a rock, where no water could naturally be.

I will stand there before you by the rock at Horeb.
Strike the rock, and water will come out of it for
the people to drink.

—Exodus 17:6

And God will supernaturally provide what we need in
the way of provision, including food, shelter and clothes.

Your clothes did not wear out and your feet did
not swell during these forty years.

—Deuteronomy 8:4

Because of our baby faith in the wilderness, God
extends much grace. Though the children of Israel continually cursed God, murmured at Moses and said they
wanted to go back into Egypt, God continued to feed,
clothe and provide them with free food and water—
miraculously.

This is why the wilderness experience is characterized by miracles. The Israelites may have blundered around in the barren desert forty years while the Promised Land was only a month's walk away—but their needs were always met. And the same is true of the process of every type of salvation.

This principle is also true in the process of personal or national salvation and redemption. When you are first set free from the slavery of sin, there will be a lot of miracles in your life, ministry, church and business. Many people start a business and experience sudden prosperity. They get so excited in the first three months that they think millions are coming. But as time progresses, and they fail to mature in the things of God, the miraculous provision slowly dries up, and they soon wonder how they are going to keep the business open.

Do you remember when you first received salvation? You wanted to save the whole world, right? You had just been through a miracle experience, and you were so excited. You would pray for toothpaste, and it would come in the morning. God did everything for you. But now that you've been saved for several years, you wonder if God even thinks about your teeth.

When you are in God's wilderness experience you will always have free provisions. He will provide for you and take care of everything you need. It is during this period that many new converts think of God as Santa Claus. So did the Hebrew children in the wilderness.

You are sponsored by God in the wilderness. It is there that God underwrites everything, supplying every need—without accountability. And He will do it despite any sinful tendencies you drag in from the dark days of Egypt.

God will feed you in the wilderness even if you murmur. God will bless you even if you sin. God will supply for you. He will take care of you even if you curse Him when you're walking out those early days. If you backbite, if you have jealousy, if you get involved in detestable things, God will still feed you and take care of your needs. Why? To keep His Word and integrity, to show you His nature and to confirm His love for you. However, most importantly, He gives you time and opportunity to renew your mind and change your slave spirit.

Perhaps you have been sinning, yet God has been blessing you. You've been squealing and squawking, and God has still been blessing. Why? Take a look around you. Do you see sagebrush and sand? Yes, you do, because you are in the wilderness. You are still a child growing up. Perhaps you've only been saved for a short time. God is still blessing you even in your sin. You are His young child, and despite your playing around, He is blessing you.

Wilderness people have been delivered from bondage, but they are not yet set free. *The wilderness is a place of preparation for your freedom.* The day will come when your miracles will cease, and you, by faith, will need to roll up your sleeves and start working out your salvation as a partner with God.

No matter what you think God wants to do with your life, no matter how many good things He has promised you, He will qualify you for them before He gives them to you. This is what the wilderness is for. It is a place of testing. *God will qualify you for the promise. The wilderness will qualify you for Canaan.*

God doesn't trust people He has just delivered—people who are still lazy and spiritually irresponsible.

They don't know the Bible yet, so they can't manage effectively. They aren't creative or self-motivated in the things of God. They can't handle spiritual pressure, the struggles of life, the difficulties of living or the challenges of freedom outside of the oppressor's control. They constantly want others to take care of them. God won't allow that spirit to enter Canaan. Read His words to Moses concerning why He took the Israelites to the desert wilderness first:

> If they face war, they might change their minds
> and return to Egypt.
>
> —EXODUS 13:17

Verse 18 says, "So God led the people around by the desert road toward the Red Sea. The Israelites went up out of Egypt armed for battle."

Some of you are asking God to take you into what He showed you as your purpose. You want to open that business now. You want to start that school now. You want that ministry right now. But God may be telling you that He can't trust you with a business because you haven't learned how to manage your own life yet. So He is going to keep you in the wilderness until He can grow you up and teach you to manage.

Remember, God requires management. It is in the wilderness that God reveals His love. But one day, across Jordan, He will give you a talent. And those who learn to manage will successfully trade. The principle is: *Promise demands preparation.*

There are many people who are in ministry today who weren't placed there by God. God hadn't graduated them from Sinai, but they bought business cards anyway. That's why they are causing so much trouble in the church—messing up, making mistakes, falling down. They gave themselves titles without passing God's wilderness test.

God will never give us what He hasn't qualified us to manage. So we have wilderness babies stumbling around in the promised land acting the part, raising money and living like the devil. God wants to bless us with what He promised, but it is the wilderness life that He has sanctioned that qualifies us for His entry to Canaan (freedom).

THE WILDERNESS TEST

WHEN YOU ASK God to fulfill His promise to you, you are simply asking Him to put you in class. The unspoken part of your prayer is, "Train me for it." If you ask God for something great, you also ask Him for great tribulation, testing, classroom experience and great wilderness challenges. These all qualify you for the answer that's on the way. If you try to bypass these maturing, confirming experiences, you make yourself "giant prey"—because Canaan will only bow to a mature child of God. (See Numbers 14.) Canaan (freedom) demands character, and character is built through time, tests and discipline.

So when you pray, wilderness pilgrim, make sure you understand that God will prepare you for the answer to that for which you are praying. You may want to restrict your prayer to "the will of God" as He knows it for you at the time, because if you start asking for things for which you aren't qualified, He won't give them to you. Instead, He wants to qualify you, and the qualifications may be so rough that you may tell Him to forget it.

Whatever God promises you, He will qualify you for.

I know I would have probably told God to forget it if He asked me to go forward into certain areas of my ministry before I was qualified. Today I oversee one of the only chartered Christian organizations that is represented in the United Nations. If God would have told me to start moving on this before I was qualified, I probably would have embarrassed Him and lost my credibility around the world. We are also on international TV and receive many speaking invitations that never would have come if I bought my business cards while still wandering in the wilderness. I had to trade with my talents before God would open those fruitful doors. And the same is true for you.

Remember, the journey from Egypt to Canaan should have taken the camp of the Israelites about forty days. After they left Mt. Sinai, where God called Israel to worship and Moses received the Law, the people walked a large circle in the wilderness before reaching Kadesh Barnea, where they sent out a spying party into the Promised Land. But ten of the twelve spies weren't ready for entry, and they came back with a bad report:

> But the men who had gone up with him said, "We can't attack those people; they are stronger than we are."
>
> —NUMBERS 13:31

The report was so deadly to those who heard it that they banded together and said, "We should choose a leader and go back to Egypt" (Num. 14:4).

Because of the influence of these ten unprepared spies, it took forty long wandering years to finally cross over the Jordan. The ten spies—and everyone they influenced—had to die in the wilderness before their children could enter into the Promised Land.

The Bible says the Israelites kept failing the class. They couldn't graduate, and because they couldn't graduate, God kept taking them back to the same lessons.

Some of us have experienced that. We fail. We avoid responsibility. We sidestep the challenges. We take a shortcut through the training and end up right back where we started, marching in circles with a hope of God, but living in rebellious defeat.

We all try to avoid some trials. But God won't allow us into His promised land without learning the lessons that trials are meant to teach. Why? Because God wants mature people. *The wilderness life trains us to live in freedom.*

God isn't going to take you to Canaan until He's satisfied that you've learned the lessons in Sinai. Now I know this conflicts with some popular church teachings, but the preparation for true freedom is tribulation and tests. God will always take you through a wilderness experience to mature you. So we must learn our lessons.

THE HEAVY BURDEN OF FREEDOM: LEARNING THROUGH WILDERNESS TESTS

IT IS IN the wilderness that God provides for and sponsors you so you can develop your ability to respond in freedom. There is a heavy burden in freedom for which we must be conditioned before God will pass us on our test. God will bless you during this season even though you are playing around and acting immature, but the blessing isn't permanent.

When you reach the Jordan River, some changes will have to take place. God will want a new response from you. He will want you to show Him that for which you are capable of being responsible. He will demand responsibility. In essence, the purpose for the wilderness is to condition us for Canaan. In fact, deliverance is not freedom. Rather, it prepares us for freedom. God will say, "Either you die on this side in the wilderness, or you change before you go across this water. Change now, or you will die in the wilderness."

> The LORD said to Moses, "How long will these people treat me with contempt? How long will they refuse to believe in me, in spite of all the miraculous signs I have performed among them?...As surely as I live and as surely as the glory of the LORD fills the whole earth, not one of the men who saw my glory and the miraculous signs I performed in Egypt and in the desert but who disobeyed me and tested me ten times—not one of them will ever see the land I promised on oath to their forefathers. No one who has treated me with contempt will ever see it."
>
> —NUMBERS 14:11, 21–23

God told Moses that the people were stiff-necked. They hadn't changed, so He kept them in the wilderness to die over a period of forty years. Sounds horrible, doesn't it? The Bible says they died in the wilderness because they didn't pass the test to cross the river (Josh. 5:4–6).

If you die in the wilderness, you'll never experience what He had planned for you. You will make it into heaven, but life on earth will be thirsty, dry and miserable. Let us learn our lessons in the wilderness so we can handle the responsibility of Canaan. The principle is: *Transformation is more important to God than relocation. Mental freedom is more important than physical freedom.*

GETTING READY TO ENTER CANAAN

CANAAN REPRESENTS YOUR promise, dream, vision, destiny and desire. Canaan is your preferred future. Every human and nation has a Canaan. *Canaan is God's predetermined purpose for your life.* In essence, Canaan represents God's will.

When it is time to enter Canaan, God will do a couple of things. First, you will have to be *circumcised.*

> At that time the LORD said to Joshua, "Make flint knives and circumcise the Israelites again."
> —JOSHUA 5:2

Circumcision is a "type" that depicts both a *distinction* and a *departure*. It distinguishes one's uniqueness from others and one's departure from an old way of life into a new lifestyle. Circumcision means God will cut off the last remaining binding, thinking pattern or memory from the wilderness, or Egypt. He doesn't want you to carry anything from your past into the future. Those habits that you developed in Egypt or the desert have to go before entering in. The great apostle Paul tells us in Romans 2:29 that New Testament circumcision is not the literal cutting away of human flesh, but of the heart. In Colossians 2:11, he likens it to "putting off the body of the sins of the flesh, by the circumcision of Christ" (NKJV). It is essential to note that the word *heart* used here literally means subconscious mind. It refers to mental conditioning.

But God couldn't circumcise the memories and habits of Israel's rebellious parents, so He raised up their children to enter Canaan instead. Any person, community or nation that does not experience a mental transformation will not experience the fullness of their potential and destiny. Why? *Because destiny demands a mentality.*

> The Israelites had moved about in the desert forty years until all the men who were of military age when they left Egypt had died, since they had not obeyed the LORD. For the LORD had sworn to them that they would not see the land that he had solemnly promised their fathers to give us, a land flowing with milk and honey. So he raised up their sons in their place, and these were the ones Joshua circumcised.
>
> —JOSHUA 5:6–7

Not one of the murmuring Hebrews who kept Egypt in their hearts was allowed to enter Abraham's Promised Land. The promise had been spoken, but they weren't ready to fulfill it to the end. Only those who had no experience or memory of slavery were allowed to enter in. Joshua and Caleb were the only exceptions, because they understood their responsibility and the opportunities that awaited them on the other side of Jordan.

Nothing in the world can corrupt Canaan more than Egyptian-slavery thinking. So God wanted Israel to have a new life, new attitude and new habits. He wanted everything new in His new land. And He wants the same thing of you. *Canaan demands conversion.*

It is in the wilderness as you draw near to God in thanksgiving for your deliverance that He expects you to grow in renewing your mind to the realities of His new life. It is there that God wants to circumcise your appetite for Egypt. If you long for your old life, God won't take you forward into His land of milk and honey. So the responsibility for your freedom is completely up to you. In essence, the enemy of Canaan is Egypt. *The enemy of true freedom is a slave mentality.*

God will never allow you to become all you were born to be until you are sick of being what you were. You will never progress to God's dream for your life until you hate the nightmare in which you were living. We must hate whom we used to be and completely abandon our past before God can make us whom He wants us to be. Remember—*mental transformation is more important than physical relocation.*

Some people still dream about whom they used to be. They do the same things they used to do with old Egyptian friends. They still pass certain Egyptian hangouts and slow down. They still desire Egyptian food.

Nothing changes until your mind changes. This is why the Creator can't trust many of us with the dream He has for us. Most of us are still thinking about Egypt, and God will keep us in that desert—twenty, thirty or forty years if we refuse to change. Many sit in a church pew on Sunday morning with Sinai's sand in their shoes as the minister preaches about Canaan. They go home after service and murmur over his message, because that's what you do when you live in the wilderness.

The Israelites wanted to go back to Egypt to their pots of meat, onions and garlic (Num. 11:5). The familiar tastes of Egypt that had pleased them for four hundred years kept them from acquiring Canaan's new taste of milk and honey.

COME OUT AND BE SEPARATE

> Therefore come out from them and be separate, says the Lord. Touch no unclean thing, and I will receive you. I will be a Father to you, and you will be my sons and daughters, says the Lord Almighty.
> —2 CORINTHIANS 6:17–18

The way God dealt with Israel is the way He will deal with us. If you are ever going to live fully the life God wants for you, you will have to change your diet. You will have to come out of Egypt and be separate. Your taste buds will have to change.

What makes life exciting for you? Do you still have a taste for liquor and drugs? Do you still drop into Pharaoh's discos and pubs? Do you still entertain thoughts of fornication and pornography? Do you dream of milk and honey while eating garlic and onions? If so, you have to change your diet, because destiny determines diet, and you eat what you want to become.

When our taste buds change, so does our diet. What is your desire toward the Word of God? Does His Bible truth excite you? Do you get up in the morning and say, "Wow, I can't wait to read the Bible!"? If so, your tastes are changing, and the wilderness is waning. Canaan lies over the Jordan, and your foot is ready to step in. What about the books you read, movies you watch, clubs you join and the friends you keep? Are they Canaan conscious?

If it is still tough to go to a prayer meeting—if the

Holy Spirit has to rebuke you and angels have to appear to get you in the door—then you haven't acquired a taste for the things of God.

If you're still thinking about onions and garlic, you can't handle milk and honey. Now there is a strange food combination. If you ate onions and garlic with milk and honey, your taste buds would rebel, and your stomach would get sick. That's what happens when you keep a taste for the food of Egypt and Canaan both—you get sick. *New desire, new destiny!*

God prefers that you be in Egypt or Canaan, because once in Canaan, Jesus demands complete commitment from His church. "I know your deeds," He told the Laodicean church in Revelation 3:15–16, "You are neither cold nor hot. I wish you were either one or the other! So, because you are lukewarm—neither hot nor cold—I am about to spit you out of my mouth." And Laodicea's word is our word in today's modern church.

God cringes at the taste of mixed milk and garlic. So you must decide where you are going to live—Egypt or Canaan, slavery or freedom. God doesn't want anything you experienced in slavery to be dragging behind you when you cross the Jordan. He wants everything that oppressed and suppressed you to be cut off in circumcision so you can cross over in a different mentality. *Remember, you cannot drive into the future by looking in the rearview mirror.*

The adults in Israel who were delivered from Egypt didn't make it to the Promised Land. It was their children, the ones who were born in the wilderness, who were trained to go into Canaan. It took God an entire generation to wipe out of their minds the influence of

Egypt. God didn't allow the parents into Canaan because they had Egypt in their minds. They had been mentally conditioned by 430 years of slavery. They wouldn't be transformed mentally. So as hard as it may sound, one of the best things God could do to move His plan along was to make sure they stayed and died in Sinai's desert sands. *Remember, wearing a crown doesn't make one think like a king.* The wilderness is God's classroom for training for Canaan. *Freedom demands preparation.*

LEADERSHIP HELP

ANOTHER THING GOD will do in preparation for crossing the Jordan is give you a human mentor to lead you into preparation for freedom. The person God puts in your life will be hard on you. He will force you to grow, because his job is to prepare you to live in freedom. Moses was Israel's mentor, and it is ironic that his hardness was the very thing that kept him from personally crossing the Jordan. When he complained bitterly about the people's slave mentality and hardheartedness, God judged him for lowering himself to the murmurers' level. Shouting out in anger over the people's rebellious hearts, he smote a rock for water instead of obeying God's command to simply speak to it.

> He [Moses] and Aaron gathered the assembly together in front of the rock and Moses said to them, "Listen, you rebels, must we bring you water out of this rock?" Then Moses raised his arm and struck the rock twice with his staff. Water gushed out, and the community and their livestock drank. But the LORD said to Moses and

Aaron, "Because you did not trust in me enough
to honor me as holy in the sight of the Israelites,
you will not bring this community into the land I
give them."

—Numbers 20:10–12

The purpose of teaching and training is not just for
information; it is for transformation. We are transformed by the renewing of our minds. But it was Moses
who led in integrity and trained Joshua to finish the job.

This training is so important to the Creator that if
you do not graduate from the wilderness school of
Sinai, He will never allow you to enter the fullness of
your purpose and destiny in Canaan.

THE CANAAN PHASE

The final phase of freedom can come only inside the bor-
ders of the promised land. God kept the children of
Israel in the wilderness for forty years because of their
irresponsibility to take Him at His word. But He kept
them alive long enough to bear the next generation,
That new generation, along with those twenty years old
and younger, could be trained by Joshua and Caleb to
possess their Promised Land. Freedom is not just a
right; it is a privilege. *Freedom is an attitude, and it is
not guaranteed; it must be earned.* Freedom is a heavy
responsibility.

UNDERSTANDING FREEDOM

After the death of Moses the servant of the Lord,
the Lord said to Joshua son of Nun, Moses' aide:
"Moses my servant is dead. Now then, you and all

these people, get ready to cross the Jordan River into the land I am about to give to them—to the Israelites."

—JOSHUA 1:1–2

Moses delivered the people from slavery, but Joshua would be God's freedom fighter. When you go through the Jordan River, God will be with you, but it is then that He will expect you to put down your manna bag and pick up your sword. Once you cross the Jordan, God will always have higher expectations of you than He did when you were in the wilderness. God's word to Joshua is our word today: "No one will be able to stand up against you all the days of your life. As I was with Moses, so I will be with you; I will never leave you nor forsake you" (Josh. 1:5).

The problem so many have is that they forget God is with them. They don't spend time with Him, so His presence isn't sensed. We must never forget that God is with us. We must come to Him as our Father every day. He is greater than any oppression experienced in the past, and He will never leave or forsake us. Everything He has promised, He will bring to pass. This remains the same. But on the other side of the Jordan, God expects us to roll up our sleeves and get to work. He deals with His promised land people much differently than He does with wilderness folk.

God told Moses to part the Red Sea with a piece of wood. But with Joshua, God told the Israelites to walk through the water. With Moses, God gave food from heaven. With Joshua, God told them to plant their own corn. With Moses, God gave the people water from a rock when the people were thirsty. Those who entered Canaan with Joshua were told to dig their own wells.

There was, and is, a distinct difference between Moses and Joshua. *Moses was a deliverer, while Joshua was a freedom fighter.* Moses' assignment was to deliver Israel from physical oppression. Joshua's assignment was to lead them into the Promised Land, and consequently into their freedom from mental oppression.

God was the same God, but the phase of life for Israel had been upgraded to the next level. Moses' group received God's miracle power; the people under Joshua were commanded to participate in becoming a part of His miracle power.

When it's time to enter freedom, the seas of life won't open any longer by themselves. When I was in college, I would pray, and tuition money miraculously came. When I prayed, God also fed and clothed me. But after I graduated, He said, "Go to work. If you don't work, you don't eat." He was the same God after graduation, but now I had been promoted to the next level of life—the level of responsibility.

Once you enter the promised land, God doesn't independently open the seas. You have to "get your feet wet," as we say. Joshua had to tell the people to put their feet in the water. They had to use faith. "I'm not sure this is going to work," some of them may have said, "but God told me to put my foot there. So I'm going to put in another step."

When you are grown, God makes you a part of the miracle. Joshua had taken over after Moses died, and Israel was in a different era. God told the new leader, "Do not let this Book of the Law depart from your mouth; meditate on it day and night, so that you may be careful to do everything written in it. Then you will be prosperous and successful"(Josh. 1:8).

"Moses sanctified you in the wilderness," God was saying in essence, "but in Canaan you have to sanctify yourselves. Now it's time to work out your own salvation. Now you must be responsible for knowing My Word yourself. No one will watch over you here to see if you are sneaking around sinning. No one will check up on you to see why you haven't come to church. It's growing-up time. Welcome to Canaan. Here, grab a shovel, pick and sword. It's time to become responsible. It's time to go to work."

Responsibility is the prerequisite for freedom. Therefore, the principle of freedom is responsibility, because freedom demands it.

BE STRONG AND COURAGEOUS

TO BE RESPONSIBLE in our calling, we must know who we are in order to be strong. God's first admonition to Joshua was, "Be strong and courageous, because you will lead these people to inherit the land I swore to their forefathers to give them. Be strong and very courageous" (Josh. 1:6–7) Freedom demands more strength than slavery.

God wanted Joshua to know that the inhabitants of their Promised Land were going to resist him so badly that he would need every ounce of strength he had. God never told Moses to be strong. Yet, this was God's first command to Joshua: "Be strong!" And this is what God is commanding the church today. Freedom demands personal strength and courage because freedom demands discipline.

This is the hour God is calling religious people to cancel their "Bless-Me" club memberships. God isn't giving us anything we "claim" anymore. We are out of the miracle wilderness of the Charismatic movement, and He is calling us to be strong. God is saying that now is the time to roll up our sleeves, dig our wells and take the land. Some of us have crossed over Jordan, but many others are dying in the wilderness with our Bless-Me club memberships and lazy lifestyles. *Take responsibility for your own destiny.*

> Have I not commanded you? Be strong and coura-geous. Do not be terrified; do not be discouraged, for the LORD your God will be with you wherever you go.
>
> —JOSHUA 1:9

To experience true freedom we must understand the difference between freedom and deliverance and em-brace the reality that freedom demands personal and corporate responsibility. This principle is to be applied to individuals, organizations, communities and nations.

God also wanted Joshua to know that some things ahead were going to be frightening. He wanted him to know this to inspire his courage. And the same is true for you. God will show you things that will frighten you when you grow up. He will give you something He knows you can handle, but your mind won't be able to believe it. So be not afraid of fear, because fear is the soil of courage. *Courage is not the absence of fear, but the freedom to face it.* Fear is necessary for coverage.

God's courage comes when fear arrives, so He wants a people who will run toward the battles and challenges of life. It is then that He infuses us with His courageous abilities and peace. In God's mind, challenges are only opportunities to exercise our potential.

Following the Israelites' miraculous rescue from Egypt, God kept Israel safe and provided for them miraculously, just as in the desert. That is the wilderness experience—a total miracle. The Egyptians all drowned in the Red Sea. But when the Israelites crossed over Jordan, the first thing they saw was Jericho. Now it was time to get out their swords and make this victory happen. Earlier they had merely watched as God sent the plagues, opened the sea and rained down the manna. Now they were a part of the miracle. Now they had to roll up their sleeves and act upon God's Word.

NEW RESPONSIBILITIES

IN THE CASE study of Israel's deliverance from Egypt, Canaan stands as a symbol of freedom and destiny. The watchword for Canaan is *responsibility*, because freedom demands responsibility. Israel was camped inside the Promised Land on the plains of Jericho when its new era began. And when it did, and when they began to eat from the produce of the land, their miraculous food supply suddenly stopped.

> The day after the Passover, that very day, they ate some of the produce of the land: unleavened bread and roasted grain. The manna stopped the day after they ate this food from the land; there was no longer any manna for the Israelites, but that year they ate of the produce of Canaan.
> —JOSHUA 5:11–12

From that time forward, the Israelites were expected to eat what the land of Canaan produced. The bread of freedom is baked by the burden of responsibility.

No More Manna

BECAUSE OF THE promised land responsibilities into which God is calling His twenty-first-century church forty years beyond the Charismatic renewal, He is bringing us to a place today where He is cutting off the manna. For some the manna has already been cut off, and they think God has left. One day everything started going wrong, so they suddenly wondered what they were doing wrong. They thought it was the devil, or that God didn't work miracles anymore. But it was God, wanting them to grow up.

Entire churches are still trying to live in the miraculous wilderness of the fifties. Back then, all you had to do was plant a tent, invite the people and miracles exploded when God showed up. But since then, God has been teaching us in His miraculous wilderness to grow up in the truth of His Word. Some have been doing it, but others haven't. They long for the lazy days when all they had to do was simply show up.

God wants His Word to be clear today. "I am still with you. But no more manna. No free food. It's time to come out of your comfortable front rooms and accept your responsibility as My servants, so I can bless the work of your hands. It is time to move from wonders to work. It is time to mature. Maturity is characterized by responsibility."

The LORD your God has blessed you in all the

work of your hands. He has watched over your journey through this vast desert. These forty years the LORD your God has been with you, and you have not locked anything.

—DEUTERONOMY 2:7

When the manna stopped across Jordan, so did the miraculous water and the miraculously preserved clothes. Everything stopped when they began to partake of the fruit of the Promised Land. Now they were to become faith partners in God's miracles. Now they were to grow into their responsibilities of possessing the Promised Land.

If you have been struggling in the wilderness, I hope the truth in this chapter has spoken to you. *God doesn't do things the same way in Canaan as He does in the wilderness.* This is important, because people who don't understand this think God has left them. Many don't make it out of the wilderness phase because they refuse to grow. You may be one of them. Maybe you've been wondering why God stopped moving in your life last year—or many years ago. He has not stopped moving. He is now wanting and expecting you to move, because destiny demands action.

When Joshua led the people into Canaan, the Hittites, Amorites and Canaanites were there to be contended with. Though the land had been promised, they had to take responsibility to fight for what was already theirs. So will you in God's land of milk and honey.

The victories you are believing for will come, but you have to fight for them, because it is responsibility time now. The days of free manna, free clothes and water from

150

the rock may be gone. But that's all right. You can dig your well now and grow your own food, because God is saying, "It is responsibility time." This is also true of nations. National independence does not guarantee freedom; it only proffers deliverance from imperialism. The spirit of industry, work and responsibility determines the success and development of a delivered nation.

The price of freedom is spelled R-E-S-P-O-N-S-I-B-I-L-I-T-Y. But are you willing to pay it? Are you ready to put down your Tinkertoys and report to God's job? Good. Now keep on reading, because life across Jordan is exciting and full.

> **The most pathetic person in the world is someone who has sight but has no vision.**
> —HELEN KELLER

PRINCIPLES OF FREEDOM

CHAPTER 6
WILDERNESS PEOPLE

1. A promise gives birth to vision. Promises give birth to faith.
2. A divine promise is more powerful than your predicament.
3. The wilderness is a place of preparation for your freedom.
4. God will qualify you for the promise. The wilderness will qualify you for Canaan.
5. Promise demands preparation.
6. God will never give us what He hasn't qualified us to manage.
7. The wilderness life trains us to live in freedom.
8. Transformation is more important to God than relocation. Mental freedom is more important than physical freedom.
9. Canaan is God's predetermined purpose for your life.
10. Destiny demands a mentality.
11. Canaan demands conversion.
12. The enemy of true freedom is a slave mentality.
13. Nothing changes until your mind changes.
14. You cannot drive into the future by looking in the rearview mirror.
15. Wearing a crown doesn't make one think like a king.
16. Freedom demands preparation.
17. Freedom is an attitude, and it is not guaranteed; it must be earned.
18. Responsibility is the prerequisite for freedom.
19. Courage is not the absence of fear, but the freedom to face it.
20. God doesn't do things the same way in Canaan as He does in the wilderness.
21. The victories you are believing for will come, but you have to fight for them, because it is responsibility time now.

SEVEN

WALKING THE WILDERNESS WITH CHRIST

It's OK to lend a helping hand—the challenge is getting people to let go of it.

GOD SPOKE HIS promise to you and me before we were born into life. His Word is eternal, and His promise is surely giving health and prosperity to those who choose life. But we must do the choosing—we must be willing to work. I'm not talking about "works" in the context of earning our way into God's favor. This, as I have mentioned, is absolutely impossible. Ephesians 2:8–9 declares:

> For it is by grace you have been saved, through faith—and this not from yourselves, it is the gift of God—not by works, so that no one can boast.

I'm talking about reporting for duty, being led and used as God's mouth, legs and arms. In Egypt you were oppressed; in the wilderness you were miraculously blessed; but once you get to Canaan, it's time to grow up

153

and serve. Egypt is forced labor; Canaan is self-initiated work by choice. Egypt is punishment; Canaan is discipline. Egypt is pressure; Canaan is responsibility.

LIFE BETWEEN THE WATERS

WHEN THE CHILDREN of Israel came from Egypt, the first body of water they encountered was the Red Sea. They crossed it and entered the wilderness. Then they wandered the Sinai Desert until every Hebrew with a slave mentality was dead and gone. Ahead of them was a second body of water—the Jordan River. Preparation for freedom must take place between these two bodies of water.

I believe with my whole heart that the church today is living on the banks of the second body of water, the Jordan. We have been walking back and forth on its Sinai Desert banks, skipping rocks off its surface, but we haven't yet placed our foot in its waters. So we haven't entered yet.

There is no salvation in the literal story of the Israelites, but the Israelites do serve us as a type. Salvation comes through another wilderness wanderer, God's Son, Jesus Christ. Jesus also went into the wilderness to be tempted and tested, passing every test. And He did it in the forty short days that Israel would have been in the desert if they could only have passed their tests. The life of Jesus serves as a prototype for the journey of all human experience from oppression to freedom.

In this chapter we will learn from the life of Jesus, who crossed through the Jordan in baptism, went out to the wilderness for testing, then returned in the power of God's Spirit to lead you and me into the promised land.

JESUS: FREEDOM'S SHINING EXAMPLE

JESUS IS MANKIND'S ultimate example of responsible freedom in living. As a man, He walked the earth with the same needs of any human being. He was born in bondage to human subjection. He was born under Caesar's domination and oppressed by the Romans. He grew up under that oppression in wisdom and favor with God. As our example, Jesus developed Himself intellectually in the local synagogue. Then, at the age of thirty Jesus was ready to enter His ministry. To enter it, He went to the first river, the river Jordan, to be baptized by John.

> Then Jesus came from Galilee to the Jordan to be baptized by John. But John tried to deter him, saying, "I need to be baptized by you, and do you come to me?" Jesus replied, "Let it be so now; it is proper for us to do this to fulfill all righteousness." Then John consented.
>
> —MATTHEW 3:13–15

Jesus knew He had to go through water like everyone else. So He went to the place where John was. When He arrived, John asked to be baptized by Him—but Jesus directed the prophet to fulfill all righteousness. When Jesus came out of the water, He received the Holy Spirit as God thundered overhead, "This is my Son, whom I love; with him I am well pleased" (v. 17).

I want you to notice where Jesus went next. When the Holy Spirit filled Him, He wasn't led directly into the work of His ministry. The Spirit didn't take Him directly to the Promised Land. Instead, the Spirit took Him into the wilderness, to pass His own set of tests.

> Then Jesus was led by the Spirit into the wilderness to be tempted by the devil.
>
> —MATTHEW 4:1

Jesus was led into the wilderness to be tempted, or tested, by the devil. Just as Israel's deliverer, Moses, led the Israelites to the wilderness for testing and training, Jesus confronted the devil in the hot desert sands. And Jesus won the contest—to show us how to win. If you are facing your wilderness of challenge, remember it is preparation for freedom. If the Holy Spirit led our living example, Jesus, into a confrontation with Satan in the wilderness, God will lead you there.

Every individual, community, nation or organization must go through the wilderness of life just as Jesus did. Just thank God that everything you go through is right on schedule. Don't feel that the devil is winning or that God forgot you. Remember, you are in class. And if Jesus enrolled and graduated, you must enroll and complete your course also.

So many want to go directly to ministry or into a successful business. They want to buy those business cards with that title on them without learning the truths of responsibility, training and tests. They're not ready to live up to Joshua's Promised Land words exhorting us to meditate in the Word and act accordingly. They don't want to learn how to discipline themselves or to develop character. They would rather call a prayer meeting or a corporate fast so they can be seen up front as the "leader." Then when the tempter comes to destroy what they're doing and humiliate their efforts (and he *will* always come), they run back into the wilderness because they weren't prepared for the test of responsibility.

THREE TESTS

To DEVELOP MATURITY, character, self-discipline and integrity, everyone must pass three tests that are common to all mankind. Because God wants us to be controlled internally, He calls us while in the wilderness to pass these three responsibility tests. The testing is not forever. Jesus spent forty days, and when He was finished He had passed all three tests perfectly to serve as our example. These three tests include the areas of physical discipline, motivation and greed. These are the areas God tests in the wilderness to prepare you to cross the Jordan. Once you pass all three, you are ready to get your feet wet.

The categories of these tests fall under three headings:

1. Test for appetite
2. Test for motive, pride and fame
3. Test for greed and power

These tests are necessary because people who aren't used to power are dangerous. The same is true of people who are full of pride or can't possess their own bodies through bringing their appetites under control. These are irresponsible and dangerous people who cannot be trusted.

Let us take a look at each of the tests given to Jesus.

1. Test for appetite

> The tempter came to him and said, "If you are the Son of God, tell these stones to become bread."
>
> —MATTHEW 4:3

This first test was a temptation to self-gratification, and it dealt with our three basic appetites: food, drink and sex. No one is truly free until he has disciplined all of these areas. Let me point out that this was also the first area of testing for Israel in the wilderness. They began to cry out for food—self-gratification. They quickly forgot about the miracle of the plagues and the Red Sea and concentrated on their own self-fulfillment.

> The whole Israelite community set out from Elim and came to the Desert of Sin, which is between Elim and Sinai, on the fifteenth day of the second month after they had come out of Egypt. In the desert the whole community grumbled against Moses and Aaron. The Israelites said to them, "If only we had died by the LORD's hand in Egypt! There we sat around pots of meat and ate all the food we wanted, but you have brought us out into this desert to starve this entire assembly to death." Then the LORD said to Moses, "I will rain down bread from heaven for you. The people are to go out each day and gather enough for that day. In this way I will test them and see whether they will follow my instructions."
>
> —EXODUS 16:1–4

> The whole Israelite community set out from the Desert of Sin, traveling from place to place as the LORD commanded. They camped at Rephidim, but there was no water for the people to drink. So they quarreled with Moses and said, "Give us water to drink." Moses replied, "Why do you quarrel with me? Why do you put the LORD to the

> test?" But the people were thirsty for water there, and they grumbled against Moses. They said, "Why did you bring us up out of Egypt to make us and our children and livestock die of thirst?"
>
> —Exodus 17:1–3

One of the heaviest burdens of freedom is the self-imposed discipline you must have in the area of your appetites—food, drink and sex. Freedom demands self-control.

2. Test for motive, pride and fame

> Then the devil took him to the holy city and had him stand on the highest point of the temple. "If you are the Son of God," he said, "throw yourself down. For it is written: 'He will command his angels concerning you, and they will lift you up in their hands, so that you will not strike your foot against a stone.'"
>
> —Matthew 4:5–6

This test was a temptation for instant fame and sudden success. If Jesus had done this, He would have become famous instantly, and thousands of people in the temple courtyard would have seen this miracle and believed in Him. However, it would have canceled and bypassed the process of character formation and growth necessary to become responsible for the freedom He possessed to free others. The nation of Israel wanted to go instantly into their Promised Land of Cannan and freedom, but God required the *process* of training and development for mental transformation.

> When Pharoah let the people go, God did not lead them on the road through the Philistine country, though that was shorter. For God said, "If they face war, they might change their minds and return to Egypt." So God led the people around by the desert road toward the Red Sea. The Israelites went up out of Egypt armed for battle.
>
> —Exodus 13:17–18

To be truly free, you—and the nation—must go through the process of character development. True success is never instant.

3. Test for greed and power

> Again, the devil took him to a very high mountain and showed him all the kingdoms of the world and their splendor. "All this I will give you," he said, "if you will bow down and worship me." Jesus said to him, "Away from me, Satan! For it is written: 'Worship the Lord your God, and serve him only.'"
>
> —Matthew 4:8–10

When a man is free from the need for power, he is qualified for authority. So this test was a temptation of power and greed. Its trap demanded the sacrifice of Jesus' integrity and character for power. The Israelite community failed this test in the wilderness, because they could not submit to authority or understand it. They rebelled against authority and therefore were not qualified to possess it. Whatever you compromise to gain, you will lose.

Jesus passed all three tests in forty short days, one for each year Israel spent failing their wilderness tests. And when He had passed all three exams, angels ministered to Him. Remember, when you are free from the need for power, you are qualified for it.

> Then the devil left him, and angels came and attended him.
>
> —MATTHEW 4:11

When Jesus came out of the desert, He was anointed in the power of the Holy Spirit. He had fulfilled God's will in His wilderness tempting and successfully passed God's tests. Jesus overcame the devil to give you and me the power to overcome him, too. This was the crossing of the second river that the Holy Spirit said shall "flow out of your belly like a river." (See John 7:38.)

> Jesus returned to Galilee in the power of the Spirit, and news about him spread through the whole countryside.
>
> —LUKE 4:14

If you haven't had angels involved in your life for a long time, perhaps it is because you haven't passed any tests lately. Angels are sent to minister to those who have gone successfully through a wilderness test. They accompanied Joshua and Israel's armies into Jericho, and they accompanied the ministry of Jesus everywhere He went. God's anointing also went with them, working miracles as they served.

You may note that the full release of the Spirit took place *after* the wilderness experience. This river of anointing was the second river that ushers us into the land of freedom. Individuals, communities and nations must pass the wilderness test that leads first to independence, then ultimately to freedom.

According to God's process, you receive the anointing after you qualify for that level of ministry. But most Christians want God's angels and His anointing without going through the test.

An anointing is deposited within you as a talent with whatever you were born to do. (See Matthew 25:14–30.) But it won't develop into God's purpose for giving it until you've qualified by passing the test that builds trustworthy character in your life. Anointing is divine ability or enablement to accomplish a task or assignment. Every human possesses an anointing for his or her unique purpose and assignment.

Anointing doesn't come because you ask for it. *No matter how great your dream is, you will never fulfill it until you pass the test that qualifies you to manage the dream.* Remember, management is the key. God hands out no management degrees to those who flunk His tests. True freedom is the liberty to dominate and release your true work gift. But your full ability or anointing cannot be released or maximized until you have completed the wilderness school of self-discipline and pure motivation. *The wilderness of wonders prepares you for your work.*

After Jesus was anointed, He went directly to the synagogue, opened the scroll and read Isaiah's prophecy concerning Himself.

> The Spirit of the Lord is on me, because he has anointed me to preach good news to the poor. He has sent me to proclaim freedom for the prisoners and recovery of sight for the blind, to release the oppressed, to proclaim the year of the Lord's favor.
> —LUKE 4:18–19

It was then, after the wilderness, that Jesus crossed back over the Jordan to begin His ministry in the anointing of God's power. He cast out demons, healed the sick, raised the dead and cleansed the lepers. Then He died for our sins and redeemed us. And when we come to Him, He takes us through the same kind of wilderness testing to release our anointing for Canaan's responsibilities. Remember, Canaan is where we roll up our sleeves and get to the work of our life's calling in the power of God's Holy Spirit. It is in Canaan that we not only watch miracles happen, but we become a part of the miracle, not just the immature recipient of it. But before we are ready to enter in, we must all possess our bodies, pride and foolish desires for power. This is the purpose of the wilderness—preparation for possession.

THE CHURCH

NOW THAT WE have taken the time to discuss some of these truths, I invite you to notice how the disciples' wilderness and ministry experiences parallel the teachings in this book. Their wilderness ministry time began when Jesus sovereignly gave them God's Spirit as an unqualified wilderness gift. "He called his twelve disciples to him and gave them authority to drive out evil spirits and to heal every disease and sickness" (Matt. 10:1). These men didn't fast for it. They didn't pray or tarry for it, because the redemptive work of the cross had not yet been fulfilled. They were not yet born again, but Jesus gave them authority to minister His miraculous works and promised to meet their daily needs miraculously.

These twelve Jesus sent out with the following

instructions: "Do not go among the Gentiles or
enter any town of the Samaritans. Go rather to
the lost sheep of Israel. As you go, preach this
message: 'The kingdom of heaven is near.' Heal
the sick, raise the dead, cleanse those who have
leprosy, drive out demons. Freely you have
received, freely give."

—MATTHEW 10:5–8

This was the disciple's "unqualified" wilderness experience. He met their needs supernaturally and
empowered them to win everywhere they went. He
gave them each their talents and sent them out to trade.

I want you also to recognize in this passage that Jesus
told His disciples to go where it was safe. This was part
of their babyhood protection. He did this in principle
because in the beginning of a follower's wilderness
days, God will protect us from enemies. He won't give
or allow any difficult tasks that might discourage our
immature, irresponsible spirits.

Jesus sent the disciples to their own people because
He knew they would accept them. The Jews knew
them, so they would be easy to manage. They understood one another and shared the same culture.
Sending them out to the Samaritans or Gentiles at this
point in time would have been too traumatic. So He
sent them only to the "lost sheep of Israel." He wanted
them to start out easy to grow in faith.

Jesus will also make it easy during the first part of
your walk with Him. God will anoint you in the wilderness without qualification. During their early months in
the wilderness, the Israelite community was cared for in

every way. They were provided food, clothing, drink, guidance and leadership.

Jesus continued His instructions to His disciples by saying:

> Do not take along any gold or silver or copper in your belts; take no bag for the journey, or extra tunic, or sandals or a staff; for the worker is worth his keep.
>
> —MATTHEW 10:9–10

When you have a need in those early days, God will meet it. "Don't take any money or clothing, men. I will manage your affairs; you just enter in." Jesus pays the bills those first times He sends you out. "Here is my blessing," He lovingly tells us. "Here, have some money. I'll give you a job, here's a house, I'll give you some land. I'll give you everything free, as an unqualified gift. I will bless you because you are My children, and because I want you to manage this earth." This is necessary because in oppression, the oppressor provided all of these needs. And that produced a spirit of comfort, lack of industry and laziness. So in deliverance, provisions are made so we can learn how to work and provide for ourselves.

It is when you are ready to pass on into Canaan that your tempting and tests will increase. Some are ready sooner than others because of a mental maturity and the condition of their heart. But too many others stay in the desert and wander aimlessly, simply playing church.

> Not one of them will ever see the land I promised on oath to their forefathers. No one who has

treated me with contempt will ever see it. But because my servant Caleb has a different spirit and follows me wholeheartedly, I will bring him into the land he went to, and his descendants will inherit it.

—NUMBERS 14:23–24

Note this passage of Scripture says that this Israelite Caleb had a *different* spirit. The word *different* in this passage is not referring to the Spirit of God, but rather to Caleb's attitude and mind-set.

This wilderness principle teaches us that when the Lord sends us out the first time, He shows His power through our lives and miraculously meets our every need. There was no need for any Bible education or training. John 3:16 and your testimony is all you need.

But there comes a time when God starts pulling all this back, and we begin to wonder, *God, are You still with us?* Yes, He is, but He is working in another way. Now it is time to put on our management caps.

The time came when Jesus instructed His disciples differently than He had on the earlier occasion of sending them out:

> But now if you have a purse, take it, and also a bag; and if you don't have a sword, sell your cloak and buy one.
>
> —LUKE 22:36

This was the same Jesus who told His men in Luke 10, "Take no bag for the journey, or extra tunic, or sandals or a staff; for the worker is worth his keep." Now in Luke 22, He was near the end of His earthly ministry.

Now He told them to take a bag, a purse, a cloak and even a sword. The disciples had been maturing, because in verse 38 they said, "See, Lord, here are two swords." To this Jesus replied, "That is enough."

What does this mean? When the time comes for us to reach maturity in the Canaan land of our lives, God expects us to join in the fight as His earthly representatives. This time comes for every individual, community and nation who crosses the Jordan. We will be held accountable for taking our own purse, buying a new cloak and sharpening our battle swords.

The danger of this kind of authority and freedom is that there is no more free lunch. No more free clothes. No more free shoes. It's dangerous to be free, because you have to be responsible. The excitement of it all is the satisfaction of growing and acting in faith as you witness God change the world around you through your obedience. Freedom demands responsibility.

Do you recall when you witnessed as a new believer— and people received Jesus every day? Now when you talk to nonbelievers, perhaps they say that you're crazy. "Jesus who?" they mock. All of a sudden you become intimidated and stop witnessing because it isn't familiar any more. There were some rough Samaritans out there who started challenging your faith. You encountered other religions, such as Muslims, Buddhists, Humanists and Scientologists. They asked you how you knew your faith was true and asked you to prove Jesus is the Son of God. "Prove to me that He was raised from the dead," they started to taunt. "How do you know the Bible is true?"

The easy days of John 3:16 and your testimony were over, and you couldn't show them from Genesis through Revelation why Jesus is Lord. You couldn't open a door to lay hands on them to release a miracle into their body. You couldn't show them how the Bible's miraculous writing and compilation could get an honest seeker saved. So you became frustrated and spurted out, "If you don't want to get saved, you can go to hell!"

When you were first born again, it came naturally. People wanted to listen, and the unqualified anointing of God in your life was fresh, exciting and bold. But a year or so later it started getting harder because God wanted to use you at another, higher level.

Believers have been blessed by the Lord over the last forty years. When we said, "Oh, yes, bless me with a Cadillac," He gave us the Cadillac. When we said, "Please, bless me with a house," He gave us a house. "Bless me with food," and He gave us food. "Bless me with a spouse," and He gave us husbands and wives. We have been members of the "Bless-Me" club for four decades now while the prosperity and confession message worked, and God answered our prayers.

But have you noticed lately that God seems to be pulling all the stuff back? Our wilderness days since the 1947 to 1958 healing revivals have come to an end. Our forty years have passed since God introduced the church to His miraculous provision and power. Now it's time to cross over Jordan. God gave us time to mature; now He's going to see how mature we've become with our Cadillacs. Can we live without one for three months? Can we handle catching a bus?

God wants to know today if we are responsible enough to say, "Lord, I'll still serve You if I don't have a car. If You take my house, I'll still love You." God is seeking mature believers today who aren't interested in following Him because of what He can give, but because we love and want to serve Him. Are we willing to work for and manage the payments of our mortgage, car, business and real estate?

When we are in the wilderness, miracles are wrought beyond our understanding. But on the other side of the Jordan in Canaan we must learn how to serve, study and pray. There comes a time when God says, "Time to go to school." I know, because He did that with me. The twenty-first century is the season of Canaan, the age of responsibility, the era of work.

MANNA IS NEVER FOREVER

MANY PEOPLE MISTAKE God's anointing for skill, and they confuse God's power with training. But God will use both to mature His children, because an anointed and skillful individual, community or nation can honor Him best. When I was young in the ministry, everything was going our way. I would just breathe, a song came out and people would buy it. Hundreds of thousands of dollars came into my music group's hands. This was my wilderness experience. We just showed up, and folks showed up. Then, all of a sudden, at the peak of the ministry God told me to go to college to further my academic preparation. I said, "Are You crazy, God? I'm a hit in town."

So He told me again, "Go to school. That's enough. The anointing for this phase of your life is finished."

"Wait a minute," I said, "God, everyone likes me."

"Don't worry," He replied, "soon they are going to hate you. Go to school."

Don't ride the early wilderness miracle days until they leave you. Prepare yourself for when they will sovereignly leave. And they will, so get your training. The wilderness is training for Canaan. Manna is never forever.

God will bless the business you started, but don't let that business run down without getting some training on how to keep your business running. Go to seminars. Buy books. Learn accounting. Learn organization. Learn management. Get the training. Why? Because during the first part of your enterprise, God will bless you and make the business work with His anointing in spite of your mistakes. But when that anointing leaves, you had better have some training to keep that thing going because God is going to work differently then. He's going to demand responsibility. The anointing for miracles in the wilderness will turn to anointing for responsibility.

Let's look one last time at how Jesus' perspective changed between the first and last time He sent the disciples out to minister His Word. As we do, I invite you to put what He said in perspective with what He is saying today to the twenty-first century church.

> Then Jesus asked them, "When I sent you without purse, bag or sandals, did you lack anything?" "Nothing," they answered. He said to them, "But now if you have a purse, take it, and also a bag; and if you don't have a sword, sell your cloak and buy one."
>
> —Luke 22:35–36

Jesus is telling those of us who have been around for years that the time of our Bless-Me club days are coming to an end. As He instructed the disciples, He is also instructing us: "I've given you food, clothes, money, shelter—every resource you needed. But now you are mature, and it is time to start feeding and dressing yourselves. Now I want you to pray as I have and to recognize and obey My voice."

Jesus knew persecution was on the way, and He wanted His men to be ready for it. He also wanted them to learn how to believe for God's best when the worst was happening around them. And they did, because they crossed over Jordan, received His Spirit and turned the world upside down before they were martyred.

In the twenty-first century, God is calling you and I to pass over the Jordan of the wilderness that separates us from freedom in Canaan. If you have been living between the Red Sea and the river Jordan and your manna has run out, be of good cheer, because God still wants to bless you. Today God is saying, "There were times when you asked in prayer, and I provided. But now I want you to seek, and when you find it, knock." Why? The door's locked now. He isn't opening your doors as He once did. Now you have to push them open. Sometimes you have to pound hard and irritate them open, because now you are an adult.

God is going to make sure that those moving with Him in the twenty-first century are soldiers, not malingerers. We will have to be strong and courageous fighters, because what is coming in the last days will take some powerful people to overcome. *The twenty-first century will be one of responsibility—a century of maturity.*

LIVE OR DIE

NOW LET ME challenge your mind. In the days that are

coming, you must be tough enough to handle the giants on the other side of Jordan. God will make sure that you either develop in the coming testings or that you die under the pressures of them. Don't tell Peter, James, John or any of the other first-century apostles any of this twentieth-century Bless-Me club stuff. Don't try to tell them that God wants His children tribulation free and that persecution only comes to those who are too weak to deal with the devil. Listen to Peter's words on the subject:

> Dear friends, do not be surprised at the painful trial you are suffering, as though something strange were happening to you. But rejoice that you participate in the sufferings of Christ, so that you may be overjoyed when his glory is revealed.
> —1 PETER 4:12–13

God will refine you in the fires of the twenty-first century because the next move of God is going to demand an adult church. The world is ready for a people whose appetite for manna has been exchanged for milk and honey, whose desire for wonders has been replaced with a desire to work.

The church is two thousand years old, yet we're still bickering, divided, jealous, pouting and bouncing around from ministry to ministry. Jesus isn't coming back to marry an adolescent bride. We have laws in many nations of the world that forbid the marrying of a minor. So do you think Jesus is going to marry a kid? God wants us to settle down, grow up and realize that we are here to change the world. When we do, that's when we'll start hearing wedding bells.

I saw a study in *Charisma* magazine some years ago

about two thousand churches. They discovered that 20 percent of the people were tithing and carrying the church while the other 80 percent weren't giving. Today God is still saying, "When are you *all* going to grow up and tithe? When are you going to stop trusting in the world and simply believe My Word? Eighty percent of you are robbing Me every time you bring your paycheck home, and you're wondering why the manna dried up seven years ago? Wake up!"

The church was conceived by people who were selfishly living in sin before they became God's "called-out ones." That's what the word *church*, or *ecclesia* in biblical Greek, means—"called-out ones." God called His church out just as He called out the children of Israel. So if you are a part of His church, He has called you out personally.

God didn't call His church to go to heaven. One day we will go there, but until then we have been called out of darkness to proclaim the excellencies of our God. And when you start doing that wherever and whenever He calls you to do it, all persecution will break out upon you. You may want to break out of the desert and cross into Cannan. But with God's Canaan blessing, you will need to know how to fight. So He has had you in the desert to change your mind. Canaan is a symbol of your true freedom, destiny and purpose.

Are you having tough times? Good, you are right on target. Just be aware of the test. If it's tough for you, you are in the right classroom. God is making sure that you get Egypt out of your mind before you enter Canaan. God wants to get the taste of Egypt out of you. He wants to try your faith. He wants to work on you so that you become so abandoned to Him there isn't anywhere else but Canaan for you to go. He doesn't want you arriving at Kadesh-Barnea and cowering before the giants who roam the Promised Land. He wants Joshuas and Calebs who know that God will fight with them in taking the Promised Land. Read their words:

> The land we passed through and explored is exceedingly good. If the LORD is pleased with us, he will lead us into that land, a land flowing with milk and honey, and will give it to us. Only do not rebel against the LORD. And do not be afraid of the people of the land, because we will swallow them up. Their protection is gone, but the LORD is with us. Do not be afraid of them.
> —NUMBERS 14:7–9

The route to freedom is through the wilderness. I've been in the wilderness myself a number of times over the course of my life, and I thank God for every trial and test. Why? Because they build stamina, character, maturity, stick-to-it-iveness, faithfulness and trustworthiness in me. They have helped me grow into my different eras of responsibility. One era could not have happened if the previous one hadn't taken place. And as I look into the next few years ahead, I know more layers of responsibility will be added, because there is so much more to be done.

Every nation, individual and church has to go through the phases discussed in this chapter: Egypt, Sinai, Canaan—that's the process. So take some time to think as we close out this chapter on exactly where you are.

Where Are You?

You may be standing right in the middle of the Red Sea, watching miracles happen all around that you have nothing to do with. If so, God is doing everything because you are new in the faith. You are at the shallow shores of independence.

Or you may have just entered the wilderness. You've seen the sea crash down behind you, drowning the enemy's army, and you are having a wonderful time. You just got saved, just opened a business, just got married. You're like Miriam dancing in joy for the sea's miraculous parting. Soon you may be complaining because there isn't any food. But don't worry, God is going to provide for you, because your wilderness days are ahead.

Maybe you've been in the wilderness for some time. You may have been going through tribulations and tests, but at the same time God has been working miracles everywhere. While you have been growing and even complaining, God has been bringing miracle water out of the rock. His manna has been meeting your needs.

Have you reached Jordan? You must put your foot in to cross it. Do you wonder if God left you because His miraculous power doesn't work in your life as it once did?

Are you standing on Jordan's bank, aware that your

175

season is changing? As you read this book, do you have your purse and sword in hand?

You may have just arrived in Canaan, and have recently endured God's circumcision. You thought this was going to be great, but you're in pain. A few years ago you were bragging on how much of a man or woman of God you were, and how you were going to change the world. But you didn't transition out of the "free manna" days, and your house fell apart. You lost your job, your dog died, you broke your toe, your uncle died with cancer. "Where is God?" your heart cried. But you finally got it together, and now you're back.

For many of us, it used to be easy to believe for something, and it happened. Now we fast, and nothing happens. We pray, and nothing happens. We confess until our tongues get tired, and nothing happens. We hold on, but nothing happens. So we want to give up.

God is saying, "Don't give up. Take out your sword now. Gird up your loins now. Stand steady and listen now. Get ready to fight. Jericho is the next stop, and you are destined to win. Once you make the decision to circumcise your Egyptian thinking and make yourself available to fight, everything you've been holding on for will soon be at your fingertips. But the enemy is holding it, so you must dispossess his many strongholds in the land. Remember, I will do it with you."

Let's move on to see how God will help you "do it."

Freedom is moving from survival to stability,
from stability to success, from success
to significance.

—ZIG ZIGLAR

176

PRINCIPLES OF FREEDOM

CHAPTER 7
WALKING THE WILDERNESS WITH CHRIST

1. No matter how great your dream is, you will never fulfill it until you pass the test that qualifies you to manage the dream.
2. The wilderness of wonders prepares you for your work.
3. The twenty-first century will be one of responsibility—a century of maturity.
4. The route to freedom is through the wilderness.

EIGHT

THE PRINCIPLE
OF RESPONSIBILITY

The only place success comes before work
is in the dictionary.
—DONALD KENDALL, CHAIRMAN, PEPSI-COLA COMPANY

RESPONSIBILITY IS THE key to true freedom. Now we are
going to break down these wilderness principles to
make freedom a reality in your life. If you've been spinning your wheels in the wilderness and are tired of
living in oppression, responsibility is the answer to your
coming years in life. The prerequisite for freedom is
responsibility. What is responsibility?

Let's look at the word *responsibility*. I like to divide it
up into three parts and look at each one. This is not the
official dictionary version of the origin of the word, but
this really helps me get a grasp on its meaning.

The first part of the word *responsibility* is "re," which
means "to return to the original, to go back to the source."

The second syllable of *responsibility* is "spons." This
always reminds me of "sponsor," which means "one who
assumes responsibility to pay for another or support

another." A sponsor is a supporter or an upholder. The sponsor is the one who pays for something or who oversees and is responsible for the execution of something. A sponsor is one's source.

The final part in the word *responsibility* is "ability." Ability means "to have the power to perform whatever is required." So *ability* is strength, capacity, might and potential.

When we put the three parts of this word together, we get an interesting definition. *Responsibility* means "submitting, or returning in submission, the power given to you." It is giving account of the ability to the one who sponsored you by maximizing that potential as he demands.

For example, when your mother gave you the responsibility to clean the dishes during your childhood, she knew you had the ability to respond to her demand. So she expected you to respond to her assignment with your ability to manage the assignment. If you ran off when you were called by the kids outside for after-dinner games, when you finally returned, your daddy would probably take you out back with the responsibility to discipline you. But more importantly, you would have been irresponsible because of your neglect to respond to the ability your mother knew you had when she sponsored you to help around the house.

The same would be true with a greater spiritual impact by rejecting God's job assignment for your life to establish His will on earth. It is irresponsible to neglect His will. Never forget that God gives you the power to do things. He is the source of your abilities—and using them effectively and fully shows you are responsible.

Re-spons-[a]bility

When God gives you a seed, He doesn't want that seed back; He wants a forest. He wants you to plant and grow that seed with the ability He gave you. When God gives you something, it always contains more than is apparent. His seeds have the potential to be more than what initially appears. He gives you His seed of potential with the end product in it, and it is the end product—not the seed—that God wants back. This is the emphasis in Jesus' parable of the talents. He gives you one to manage into many. Let's look at it again.

> Again, it will be like a man going on a journey, who called his servants and entrusted his property to them. To one he gave five talents of money, to another two talents, and to another one talent, each according to his ability. Then he went on his journey. The man who had received the five talents went at once and put his money to work and gained five more. So also, the one with the two talents gained two more.
> —Matthew 25:14–17

In this powerful parable, Jesus teaches us that God is our source. It is God who sponsors us freely with our talents, gifts and abilities. It is He who gives us our dreams and purpose. After He imparts them, He doesn't want our dreams and gifts back. He wants us to develop His gifts by responding to the abilities invested in us.

To the servants who managed their dreams and abilities, the master declared, "Well done, good and faithful servant! You have been faithful with a few things; I will put you in charge of many things. Come and share your master's happiness!" (v. 23).

The third servant didn't appreciate his master's gift, and he didn't appreciate his invested abilities. So he buried his talent to hide it from all. When his master returned, he was punished severely.

> His master replied, "You wicked, lazy servant! So you knew that I harvest where I have not sown and gather where I have not scattered seed? Well then, you should have put my money on deposit with the bankers, so that when I returned I would have received it back with interest. Take the talent from him and give it to the one who has the ten talents. For everyone who has will be given more, and he will have an abundance. Whoever does not have, even what he has will be taken from him."
>
> —Matthew 25:26–29

When an investment *appreciates*, that means it grows. When we *appreciate* the gifts and dreams God gives us, we make them grow. In this parable two grew to four, and five grew to ten. But for the one who tried to give the master back his seed, his return was death. When God gives a seed, He expects a tree.

If the gifts you had last year don't grow this year, if you aren't a little wiser because of trading with your gifts, you will be held accountable for your ungratefulness to God for the gift of your talents and for the great brain He gave you.

I have come to understand the gifts and dreams God has placed within me more every year. So to help develop them, I read at least fourteen books a year. In my busy schedule, I find time before I go to sleep and at other times to read a few chapters. I have four briefcases, and in each one I have a book that I find time every day to read. I make it a goal to finish each title, so I work it into my schedule. You must constantly refine your gift.

PRIORITIZE, ORGANIZE, DISCIPLINE

MAYBE YOU'RE WONDERING how you could read that many books. I had to discipline myself to sit down, stop watching television, turn the video off, stay up a little later or get up a little earlier to read. I chose to be responsible in order to get the knowledge into my brain. This is the essence of freedom. *Freedom demands the three keys to success—prioritize, organize and discipline.*

The beautiful thing about it is, the more I learn, the more others benefit because I become a better teacher. When I get more knowledge, I can bless more people. Then more people want to hear me, and I am invited to speak in more places. So my gift expands and grows, and God opens more doors. This is the way He designed it to work. I took His talents, and I'm still trading with them.

God gave each of us a brain with one billion cells, and according to scientists, we only use 10 percent of it. Now I don't know about you, but I think that's sad. So I have decided that I'm going to make use of 15 percent of my brain. I want to live at a level above the average human being, so I trade with my talents daily. Jesus said, "To everyone who has shall more be given" (Matt. 25:29, NAS). I grow in my responsibility with every new task. How about you? Freedom makes demands on your ability. It's the nature of freedom.

Just like the servants in the parable, we will have to

return to our Source one day and say, "Look at what I did with what You gave me." The servant who received five talents didn't bring five back. That would have been irresponsible. He came back with ten, and his master was thrilled. "But the man who had received the one talent went off, dug a hole in the ground and hid his master's money" (v. 18). He came back with zip, nadda, nothing. Instead of earning a profit, he earned his master's wrath.

"You wicked, lazy servant!" said the master (v. 26). Then he said, "Take the talent from him and give it to the one who has the ten talents. For everyone who has will be given more, and he will have an abundance. Whoever does not have, even what he has will be taken from him. And throw that worthless servant outside, into the darkness, where there will be weeping and gnashing of teeth" (vv. 28–30).

There are some things God hates. And as we've seen, irresponsibly squandering our God-given abilities is definitely one of them. Jesus not only called the servant lazy and wicked, but the man was condemned to eternal damnation. Wow! Not only that, but God took the hell-bound servant's one talent and gave it—not to the one who had the four—but to the one who had the ten.

Now when I first read this parable as a young believer, I was confused. In my way of thinking then, the needs and math didn't add up. So I said, "God, wait a minute. The one who had the ten was loaded. So why didn't he give the unfaithful servant's one squandered talent to the man who had the four? At least then, he would have been a little better off with five. And the one with the ten would have still done OK, because he received two times what the other man had."

But God's Spirit is a wise Spirit. He showed me that in God's program of management affairs, the people who are busy developing their lives and going forth responsibly will always receive a huge return on their life investment. He showed me that this parable warns us all to be responsible. *If you are waiting to get blessed before you start doing something, you are going to lose what you have.*

This is management by God's book: The more you receive from the Lord, the more demands He places on you. "From everyone who has been given much, much will be demanded; and from the one who has been entrusted with much, much more will be asked" (Luke 12:48).

What have you received? If you have a voice but don't sing, you will lose your desire and talent to sing all together. You won't practice, and you won't increase in your gift. Those of you who have been given the ability to do business with an administrative mind, you need to use it. Don't be afraid to exercise it by preparing yourself for promotion—if you don't go to night school because you are too lazy, you won't remain even where you are. You will eventually lose your job. Someone else will step into your position on the way to the top while you're sitting there spinning your wheels in the desert sand of the wilderness. Got the picture?

USE YOUR ABILITIES, AND GOD WILL GIVE YOU MORE

RESPONSIBILITY PAYS GREAT dividends once we choose to walk in God's ways. When you begin to exercise and multiply what God has given you, He will bless you with more. This is why the people who seem to be getting the most are the people who are doing the most.

A pastor once asked me, "Brother Myles, why are you getting all these invitations and speaking engagements? How come no one calls me?"

"I don't know," I replied. "I never look for any invitations; I'm too busy working."

The spirit of responsibility always attracts God's blessing. Second Chronicles 16:9 says, "The eyes of the LORD run to and fro throughout the whole earth, to show Himself strong on behalf of those whose heart is loyal to Him" (NKJV). If you don't attempt things, you won't attract God. But if you try, believe me, God won't let you attempt things by yourself. Step out in faith, and you will be amazed at what is waiting for you. Tell God, "I believe I can do this thing. You can show Yourself strong through me, because You gave me the strength." I'm telling you the truth, the minute you move, good things come out of nowhere toward you. Take responsibility, and God will notice.

A LAND FLOWING WITH MILK AND HONEY— BEES AND COWS

I HOLD OUT to you the thought at this point of my writing that the twenty-first-century church today enjoys slavery more than it does freedom—even if we do so subconsciously. I used to think that slavery was nothing but people controlling my life. *Now I know that there is really no greater burden than freedom itself.* So many of our brothers and sisters are wearied in a wilderness of their own making, on a long walk to nowhere, because the heavy burden of freedom is too heavy for them to bear. But Jesus has made the offer to share His freedom yoke.

Come to me, all you who are weary and burdened, and I will give you rest. Take my yoke upon you and learn from me, for I am gentle and humble in heart, and you will find rest for your souls. For my yoke is easy and my burden is light.

—Matthew 11:28–30

God's promise of milk and honey can hold true in Canaan, but there you have to work for them. There you have to trade. You don't just dig them up and eat them like onions and garlic—the foods of slavery. You must trade for them. And when the trading is done, you will hear the master's thanks: "Well done, good and faithful servant! You have been faithful with a few things; I will give you more."

The milk and honey that await those who choose to enter God's promised land of freedom represent work. This is why God referred to Abraham's Promised Land as a "land of milk and honey." How do you spell promise? W-O-R-K!

You don't dig milk from the ground. First, you have to domesticate a cow. Then you have to feed and take care of her. Then, once all of that has been done, you are ready to milk. God may give you the cow, but the rest is up to you. You are the one who must set your alarm for 4 A.M. in the morning to milk the cows when they're ready. You are the one who must wash, keep and feed Bossy. There is no sleeping in or slacking off when you want fresh milk. Then one day, you'll need some help as you staff and hire for your dairy because of that one cow. This is how things in Canaan work. *Freedom demands work and responsibility.*

God also promises sweet honey in Canaan, but there you have to fight for it. You have to break through the angry, buzzing hive, possess that hive, put your scooper in and fill your jar. Don't think those little stingers are going to open their hive doors and roll out the red carpet. No. You have to take risks in Canaan. You may get stung on the way in, but you do end up with honey. *Freedom demands risk, courage, pain and persistence.*

DECIDE TO BE RESPONSIBLE, AND GOD WILL SEE YOU THROUGH

God has tremendous blessings just waiting for people who are willing to take responsibility for their own decisions on the other side of Jordan. He wants you to step out and believe what He has put in your heart, because God responds to your responsibility.

God is obligated to pay the bills He tells you to create. Do you need another milk machine? God will see you through. But if you don't step out in responsibility, He has no reason to finance your *nothingness*. It is when you create a need by obedience that God will meet it, because *God is responsible for responding to your responsibility. He is obligated to take care of what He tells you to do.*

Obedience is the trigger that makes God move on your behalf. You may have a business, but you are afraid to expand even though God has been saying you have the ability to do it. If the ability is present, there is no reason to worry about the resources needed for expansion. *The Source who sponsored you will sponsor the growth.* But God only sponsors what He tells His middle managers to do. So do it when He speaks, and He will bring the sponsorship.

I know about this personally. I went to the university with nothing but faith. I knew God had called me there, but when I arrived, I only had enough money for one semester of college. Once I was there, however, on the other side of the Jordan, things started happening that I didn't plan. I not only received a scholarship, but the school gave me a job. Then, after they hired me, I was given two more scholarships.

When I asked the reason why I had been awarded my scholarships, they told me it was because I had earned a 3.9 grade point average. So I didn't just get blessed because I went to school; I had to study. The next semester I worked a little harder, earning a 4.0 average, and received another academic scholarship for my obedience.

But God wasn't through honoring my willingness to grow and be used in my gifts. One day, an elderly white couple in Oklahoma heard that I was a university chaplain from the islands, and they invited me to their home group to talk a little about the Bahamas and the Caribbean.

I went there and talked to them. When I finished, the man came over and asked me if I was financially set for the next year. I told him I wasn't, and that's when God really opened His floodgates. This man told me how he and his wife had been praying that they would find a way to help someone from the islands. After I shared that night, they were convinced that I was the man God told them to help. So they took care of all of my expenses that next year.

I had never met them before, but money for my schooling had been in their bank account many years. It was just waiting for me to take the responsibility to leave the Bahamas so I could spend it on developing my God-given talents.

Responsibility will always attract resources from the Source who is the sponsor, so you can bring back the end result to Him. *Responsibility demands a response.*

THE DISCIPLINE OF RESPONSIBILITY: INTERNAL CONTROL

FREEDOM IS GOD'S blessing. Adam was commanded to have dominion over all the earth. God sets the guidelines and gives us room to move. But the choice is always ours to submit to His ways and trade where we choose. When you choose to enter His promised land and trade with your talents in freedom, you are internally controlled. God doesn't kick the walls of Jericho down; you must choose to obey, and *together* you bring them down.

In Egypt, you are externally controlled. But when you grow into the responsibility of freedom, you have to master your own life. In oppression, you have a master over your daily affairs and must obey his external laws. In freedom, you are the master and make your own laws. True freedom is the liberty to dominate the resources of earth through your gifts, self-discipline and internal management. Freedom is self-initiated work.

The wicked slave in the parable of the talents viewed his boss as an oppressor. This wicked, unfaithful servant chose to do nothing out of fear because he probably thought anything he could have made in his trading would have been taken away from him. He not only misunderstood who his master was—but he also misunderstood himself.

Remember, in oppression people are motivated by external threat. In freedom, they are motivated by internal commitment. You can tell if people are coming close to freedom because you don't have to watch them.

Instead of doing what is right because of the pressure of others, they live by principles. They obey because it's the right thing to do, not because they're fearful of disobeying. *True freedom is self-management.*

HOW FREE ARE YOU?

MOST OF US prefer to have a job rather than to create one, because when you have a job, the pressure of the time clock will wake you up. Do you think the Israelites would have marched themselves to work without the Egyptians' whips? I don't. They had been oppressed in slavery for hundreds of years, so mere survival had become their aim in life. The pressure of a supervisor will make you work. But in freedom, you are not employed; you deploy your own gifts. You have to wake yourself up. You're on your own time. You must be self-disciplined. You must set your own priorities and plan your own schedule. Simply put, in freedom you take responsibility for your own life because you are the one who determines your own destiny.

This is why very few people can sell insurance. I've seen people by the hundreds come to me and say, "I've changed my job."

"What are you doing?"

"Insurance."

I smile to myself, thinking, *He's not going to make it. I know him too well. He can't even attend church four times in a row without skipping. How will he wake up, set his own schedule, design his own day, set up his own clients, arrive on time to meet them and leave on time to get to the next appointment? This I have to see.* You really have to understand freedom to be an insurance agent.

The best test of a successful insurance agent is to pay 100 percent of his income through commissions. Most people would starve to death. So most choose to work for the set salary because they're not free enough in their thinking to work on their own time.

So if you aren't free yet, don't bother with insurance. Save the hopeful agency a lot of heartache, training and money. Wait until you're free as an individual before you take on a job like that, which demands your own planning, scheduling and prioritizing.

That's exactly what God was saying to the children of Israel: "You're not ready for Canaan, so I'm going to bury you before you mess up my business." Sinai is God's classroom of responsibility. *The wilderness is the university of work.*

KNOWING YOUR VALUE

BEFORE AN INDIVIDUAL can show the kind of confidence it takes to go forward with their talents, they must understand God's personal investment in their lives and know their self-worth. I do much work in South Africa. As you know, they have been trying to change the country's mentality in that nation since apartheid was abolished in 1994. Their free elections and majority rule were enacted following centuries of separatist oppression. But when people are treated like cattle, it affects their overall self-worth. So catching up to the reality of things will take some time. You can't legislate a good self-concept or self-worth, so I have committed myself to help in the restorative process. *Political laws and legislation cannot create self-esteem.*

Our television program is seen in South Africa every

week, and it is amazing to see the kinds of letters we receive. People write in to tell us that for the first time in their lives, they feel like somebody. They tell me that my message is different from any they have ever heard. Because I am a person of a darker pigmentation, I encourage those who are grappling with a sense of self-worth to understand how truly important they are to God.

Religion and regimes sometimes work together in oppressing nations, and this is what happened in South Africa. Apartheid was reinforced in many ways by some prevailing religious thought. And because of the oppressed sense of self-worth many were coerced into believing about themselves, thousands today are wandering in the wilderness with the same slave mentality they had under white separatist rule. But God can and will change that, and I'm doing everything I can do to help them move out of the wilderness into freedom.

Real freedom doesn't come from governments. True freedom, according to Jesus, comes from "knowing the truth." When people discover the truth about themselves in the pages of God's Word, they don't need anyone to set them free. Suddenly, they discover they are already free. We need to pray for our friends in South Africa. But we need to pray for real freedom, not just the political freedom majority rule has brought, which many don't know quite what to do with yet.

When our organization moved into our own newly built facility, it was an important announcement. Not many believed anything like that could happen in Third World countries, but it did. We experienced a miracle. We had been trading with our talents and accomplished it by our faith and belief in the vision God gave us.

The message I teach gives people a sense of self, a sense of dignity and an awareness that they have a reason for living. I remind people of their importance and purpose in life, and that Jesus Christ came to restore it.

This is part of God's "talent investment" in me. He moved me on to university from the old days of music ministry to train me to reinvest. People who have been oppressed, whether by a regime or a social system, don't need a message of salvation that will only get them to heaven. Heaven will be wonderful, but earth is where we live out our faith. People need the whole gospel—to know they have great self-worth and are valuable in the here and now. God created man to manage His affairs. So we tell people in Africa, Central America, the Caribbean and around the world that they were born for a reason, and that they are unique and irreplaceable.

Jesus came to give us back ourselves. That's what we lost. So I preach Christ and Him crucified from the lecterns and pulpits of my calling. But I go beyond His crucifixion. I go to the Resurrection and beyond the Resurrection, because Jesus was raised so we could discover who we are—that's why He came. I also seek to instill God's management principles of good business practice in corporate environments, showing business leaders of the world God's principles at work. Not long ago I was able to address the corporate heads of the Sony Corporation using one of their product manuals as an illustration to show the practicality of God's "product manual" contained in His Word. When I share at the United Nations or with world leaders one on one, it is my entrusted talent to reveal the relevance of God's Word in social and political situations. Because I have shown my faithfulness, requests for speaking engagements come in from all around the world.

God increases those who have, so when you decide to trade you better get a good schedule calendar. And you better get ready for a battery of continual tests. Freedom is discovery of your true self: your self-worth, value and self-esteem. *You are truly free when you know who you are.*

TRIED AND TESTED

As the heavens are higher than the earth, so are my ways higher than your ways and my thoughts than your thoughts.

—ISAIAH 55:9

When you are on the road to responsibility, God will take you through some tests. He will take your bread from you, but He won't allow you to starve. He will hold it just long enough until you rise above your own natural thinking. Then once you have your eyes off people and natural supermarkets, He will give you the resources to buy bread. When you know your self-worth in Him, you will also recognize that His ways are higher than the ways of the natural world.

Maybe you've been just trying to make it from one day to another, and you've been wondering why. You've been giving, tithing and praying—yet money is tight. The reason is, you have never recognized God completely as your Source. You have never arrived at the place where you say, "If God doesn't do it, it won't get done." Until you get there, you aren't free. Once you recognize God as owner of everything and your place as His middle manager, your ways will increase accordingly.

True freedom is being like Jesus, and Jesus was totally dependent upon His Father God. "For I did not speak of my own accord," are His words in John, chapter 12. "But the Father who sent me commanded me what to say and how to say it. I know that his command leads to eternal life. So whatever I say is just what the Father has told me to say" (John 12:49–50).

Jesus was, and is, totally dependent on His Father. And we should be, too. He came to earth invested immeasurably with God's Spirit and miraculous talents, and He traded with them to redeem mankind. So as we look to Him, He will use us to work with His skill. And like Jesus, we will be tested to qualify for the next level of ministry God is wanting to serve through our hands.

Jesus was tested in the wilderness, and you should expect the same, too. Don't curse every test as if it's from the devil. *No test comes unless God allows it.* God is calling us over the waters . . . over the Jordan . . . and He can't lead us there until we pass our exams. People in the church have been taught that friction, conflict or challenge is from the devil. But anyone who can read Scripture should know this isn't true, because Adam had his test right there in the Garden—in that perfectly created spot.

Testing is not a result of the Fall. The New Testament tells us to welcome tests, tribulations and challenges as friends. They don't come to destroy us. They are sent to develop and refine our faith. This is why James, Jesus' natural brother by birth to Christ's mother, Mary, wrote, "Consider it pure joy, my brothers, whenever you face trials of many kinds, because you know that the testing of your faith develops perseverance. Perseverance must finish its work so that you may be mature and complete, not lacking anything" (James 1:2–4).

God gives His re-created men and women faith that needs development, and He has designed a testing program to improve, increase and develop it. Therefore tests, tribulations and trials are a part of God's program—regardless of whether a man or women is a believer or not. Whether you are in the Garden or outside the Garden, tests are a part of life. You may not have thought about it, but the final test that brought you to faith in Jesus Christ was the last time you were tested before you believed. And the last time you were asked to show more responsibility in an area, whether in the church, in the home or on the job, God was handing you a new talent to trade with—so don't bury it. Remember, a ship in harbor is safe, but that is not what ships are for.

BEING DISCIPLINED

FINALLY, IN DEALING with the talents and responsibility with which God entrusts men and women, we absolutely have to deal with the big "D"—DISCIPLINE—because discipline is an integral part of His testing program. It is inevitable once you walk out of oppression that His discipline will start to form you for freedom. When you start trading with your talents, it will form you for success. *The wilderness is the institute of discipline.*

The Book of Hebrews tells us that "no discipline seems pleasant at the time, but painful. Later on, however, it produces a harvest of righteousness and peace for those who have been trained by it" (Heb. 12:11). That is so true. When God disciplines you, you may wonder if you did something wrong. But that may not be the case. He may, in fact, be training you for a future event you know nothing about.

For example, I told my son and daughter not long ago about something they shouldn't do.

My son protested, "But we're not doing that. Why are you talking to us about something we're not doing?"

So I told him, "I'm telling you not to do it before you do it so you won't do it."

When I said this, I heard the voice of God say to me, "That's discipline. That's how I make people responsible." God doesn't want anyone to learn their lessons "the hard way." Someone once said that experience is a good teacher, but the tuition is high. So discipline is positive, not negative. God uses it to train you for freedom. Then He continues to discipline you for continued freedom. What is discipline? Discipline is self-imposed standards and restrictions motivated by a desire greater than the alternatives.

I tell my children, "Smoking is bad for your health. Drinking is bad for your liver. Cursing is bad for your communication ability." I want them to know this so they don't smoke and drink. All of my "Don't do this and that's" probably have sounded negative throughout their formative years. But one day I know my children will recognize how positive they really were. Discipline is decisions dictated by a determined destiny. Freedom demands discipline.

You don't find many alcoholics coming out of alcohol-free homes. And you don't find too many people dying from lung cancer who grew up in smoke-free homes. So when my children go to school and get exposed to these things, I want my words and lifestyle to speak to them there. Then, when the test comes, they will have a choice to make: to follow the lies of the addicted, or agree with the discipline of their father. Instead of having to learn the hard way how bad those things are, they can agree with the words of their father and tell those dope, booze and cigarette pushers, "I don't do that. I'm partial to intelligent thought. I think regularly to organize and live out my day, and that stuff is designed to make me a stupid idiot who smells like a burnt-out warehouse. Is that what you want me to act and look like? A stupid idiot who smells like a burnt-out warehouse? What's wrong with you? I'm busy living life. I don't want any. Go away."

It is my aim to enable my children to make decisions based on discipline that first seemed like a restriction. Once the discipline is internalized, they will know the difference between nonsense and good sense. Because of discipline, they will be confident in dealing with the foolishness of the world. When they go away to college, I will rest easy in knowing they have been trained by the wisdom of discipline and that they will want God's best. Freedom is not the absence of law, but the responsible response to law. True freedom is manifested in self-discipline.

> The LORD disciplines those he loves, as a father
> the son he delights in.
>
> —PROVERBS 3:12

I can say all of this from my perspective as a father to interpret God's reasons for disciplining His people. When the Hebrews were in the wilderness, they could have heeded God's disciplined instruction and made their way to Canaan in thirty-five short days. But they resisted His words and paid the price. You see, freedom is not a reality until we learn what the wilderness is designed to teach. God wanted to teach Israel the great love He had for them and to teach them to trust in His provision. But when they received the manna, they complained and wanted quail. When Moses went up on Sinai to receive their lifestyle commandments, the people "sat down to eat and drink and got up to indulge in pagan revelry" (1 Cor. 10:7).

Don't run away from difficulty—run through it. Don't avoid challenges—take them on. They are only opportunities to handle more freedom. *A disciplined man is a free man.*

God would like to do a lot of things in your life immediately. He has more talents than you could possibly know what to do with. He dispenses them when we're ready to work His redemptive will. He would like to answer that prayer you've been praying for some time now, but you aren't ready for the answer. Remember, true freedom is not a *right*; it is a *privilege* that is earned through discipline and responsibility.

Stop to think about it now that you have recognized where you are in your own deliverance from Pharaoh's mud pits. Look around and recognize your purpose at the moment. Don't try to pray yourself out of His will. Stop asking for the garlic and leeks, and stay on that difficult job. Stay faithful so He can affect the lives He sent you there to touch. Don't quit because there is difficulty on the job. Stand up to the pressure. Stay there. Recognize your test. Seek God's discipline in prayer and study every day before you report to that factory station or desk, and He will reveal the purpose for your exam. James writes:

> If any of you lacks wisdom, he should ask God, who gives generously to all without finding fault, and it will be given to him. But when he asks, he must believe and not doubt, because he who doubts is like a wave of the sea, blown and tossed by the wind.
>
> —JAMES 1:5–6

DON'T SKIP CLASSES IN THE UNIVERSITY OF GOD

DON'T SKIP CLASSES in the university of God. God will keep taking you back and repeating the same classes, hoping that you will pass. Then, and only then, will He give you another talent. "For everyone who has will be given more, and he will have an abundance. Whoever does not have, even what he has will be taken from him" (Matt. 25:29). This is why I have learned to embrace every challenge and thank God for every friction, problem and conflict. When people say it isn't going to work, I say, "It's going to work! I'm going to irritate this thing until it moves. I won't back off!"

When I accepted the truth that challenges were positive, I began to enjoy life. When I grew to appreciate the fact that life is a classroom, every person I meet is my teacher and every experience is a lesson, my life took a different turn. I became peaceful.

But somehow we have this euphoric dream in the religious movement today that trials are evil and that there will come a day when the tough times will end. If

200

someone tells you they have no trials or tribulations, believe me, they are d-e-a-d. Everyone has them; it's just that some catalog them under the heading of "devil attack" every time. Others see them as challenges and opportunities to grow, develop and stretch.

Everything in life is designed to release the hidden, trapped potential that God has placed within you. The only way to bring it out to prove and improve it is by testing. Just getting out of bed can sometimes be a test. On some days, that just may be your talent. When it's raining or snowing outside, many won't show up for work or for church. But God knows if He can get you there, He has one more opportunity to accomplish His work.

God will prepare you for freedom, but it will cost you something—your life. Responsibility returns and submits God's dreams and abilities back to Him to accomplish His given tasks. When we do it His way, He gives us more. And before we know it, we are so busy serving His work on earth that the problems of this world get lost along the way. Problems like fear, low self-worth, helplessness, ignorance, sickness, strife, jealousy and greed get buried in our victories. Tests are passed, and promotions given; two talents turn into four, and five into eleven; old thinking changes, and new doors open. This is the fruit of responsibility, and we should be running to it. *Freedom is your destiny.*

What have you been given? It's time to get to work.

To help you push on to that next step up on the wrung of your ladder, in the next chapter we will examine the many misconceptions people have held over the years concerning freedom. This will help you identify any hindering mental roadblocks that have barred your way to success. Then in chapter eleven, after discussing our response to responsibility in Chapter 10, we will discuss the realities of true freedom to help you tear down those roadblocks.

> You never conquer a mountain.
> Mountains can't be conquered. You conquer
> yourself—your hopes, your dreams.
> —JIM WHITIAKER
> FIRST MOUNT EVEREST CLIMBER

PRINCIPLES OF FREEDOM

CHAPTER 8
THE PRINCIPLE OF RESPONSIBLITY

1. Freedom demands the three keys to success—prioritize, organize and discipline.
2. If you are waiting to get blessed before you start doing something, you are going to lose what you have.
3. The spirit of responsibility always attracts God's blessing.
4. There is really no greater burden than freedom itself.
5. Freedom demands work and responsibility.
6. Freedom demands risk, courage, pain and persistence.
7. God is responsible for responding to your responsibility. He is obligated to take care of what He tells you to do.
8. The Source who sponsored you will sponsor the growth.
9. Responsibility demands a response.
10. True freedom is self-management.
11. The wilderness is the university of work.
12. Political laws and legislation cannot create self-esteem.
13. You are truly free when you know who you are.
14. No test comes unless God allows it.
15. The wilderness is the institute of discipline.
16. A disciplined man is a free man.
17. Everything in life is designed to release the hidden, trapped potential that God has placed within you.
18. Freedom is your destiny.

NINE

RESPONDING TO FREEDOM'S CALL

You cannot escape the responsibility of
tomorrow by evading it today.
—ABRAHAM LINCOLN

SINCE RUTH AND I took that short, little flight from Israel to Cairo across the Sinai Desert, I have been impacted by the forty-year wanderings of the Israelites in that small piece of desert! How short the distance was for the community of Israel led by Moses, and how drastic it all turned out. Freedom was all around them, but it never touched their hearts. "We want to go back to Egypt where we got our three square meals a day and everyone knew exactly what was expected of him!" they cried. "What's with all of this unexpected thinking and adventure thing? We want to go home!" These were the very people whose groans for deliverance came before God's ears.

The same cries for deliverance are rising from so many corners of the world today as we progress into the twenty-first century. "What happened to the miracles? Why aren't You answering my prayers as You once did? Where's my free stuff?"

Although God sent Moses to lead Israel out, the people's minds were too oppressed to hear freedom's cry. So they danced for a while; then they cried out for a return to their former Egyptian bondage—and they died in the wilderness without inheritance or home. But it didn't stop there. Within a generation after Joshua's death, the children God raised up to enter Canaan squandered their inheritance and freely gave up their homes. Why? Because freedom is expensive. Unless every generation is trained in the discipline of God's righteousness, the tests of life will flunk you—and you'll die in the wilderness of life's harsh, desert sands.

Our generation in the church today has groaned, received deliverance and, in some cases, actually crossed over Jordan in possessing the land of God's promises. Many have moved on from their miraculous care in the wilderness to shoulder the heavy burden of freedom that Canaan requires. We have more believers in the church world today who have circumcised their hearts and are following God's leading in Canaan than any modern generation of the church.

For many of us, the great teaching brought by the Charismatic movement's apostles such as Oral Roberts, Kenneth Hagin, R.W. Shambach and many others has impacted our lives. We recognized when the manna dried up. Then we went to prayer and study, and we made our next move. But thousands of others are wandering yet in the dusty sands of Sinai, unaware of who they truly are or of the promise God has given them. They still want to go to a miracle meeting and receive everything they need through the wave of a hand.

Because so many misunderstand their responsibilities in freedom, they want to sit in their front rooms and send in a television love gift that will cure their diseased body and drop money in their hand. It may have worked right after Jesus saved their lives and miraculously led them through the Red Sea. But now they're wondering why the desert is so hot and the miracles have dried up.

I want to leave you with what I have discovered over my many years of ministry to be the main misconceptions of freedom held by both the world and the church. I offer them as informed revelation that will serve you in effecting change. In this chapter we will examine freedom's misconceptions. In the final chapter we will look once more at the truths of freedom. As you commit to a new era of prayerful Bible study and bear these facts in mind, it is my hope that they will serve you as God's disciplined wisdom, able to deliver you from the oppressor's hand into the land of true freedom.

FREEDOM IS EXPENSIVE

WHEN OUR MINISTRY headquarters in the Bahamas moved into our New Ambassador Center building on the island of Nassau, we entered Canaan. For fifteen years we moved from one rented property to another before moving up to a new facility. Once there, we wondered when "they" were going to put the ceiling up. We noticed that the floors needed tiling. Dust was everywhere. The windows needed cleaning, and the fans were making noise. We also needed furniture, lawn mowers, tractors, light bulbs, bathroom tissue, water, electricity and our own telephone. "Help, God, help!" we cried.

We were being circumcised. The last murmuring spirit was being cut out of our hearts. God was cutting off the last memory of Egypt and its bondage. Today we have been digging our own prophetic wells and planting our fields for a number of years, and it is a wonderful confirmation in knowing that faith brought us there. God has blessed us in the land. We are touching the Third World, America and Europe in a blitz of exciting zeal. But it would never have happened if we did not learn how to dig our own wells.

When you read the Book of Judges, you will see how Egypt's mind-set crept back in, and the land was lost. The responsibility of freedom is always ours to bear.

Let me remind you that freedom is expensive. It doesn't come cheaply, and it must be protected at all costs. People are crying out for freedom today around the world. The Third World countries have been crying out for it for hundreds of years—"Freedom!" Most of us have received it. Colonialism in the Caribbean fell apart in the twentieth century because the people cried out for it to end. My country of the Bahamas was one of those countries.

But when we say we want freedom, we have to realize what we're asking for—RESPONSIBILITY. So we must consider the principles of freedom before we cry out for it. The dynamics and cost involved in freedom must be comprehended to be prepared for freedom's rewards.

When you say you want freedom, you say you want "talent-trading" management. But few people in the world or church truly understand this. I used to think I knew what freedom was, yet it was my very concept of freedom that kept me in bondage. My old wilderness days of playing music and getting paid handsomely for it with little, if any, effort gave me the impression that freedom consisted of popularity and easy success. Just as Jesus sent out the disciples the first time, I took no money bag and carried no sword because those easy, early days of music ministry had been prepared by the Lord to keep me safe.

God was sending the manna and bringing water forth from the rock. So I traded with my talent. Then one day we reached the edge of Canaan, and as the Jordan rushed before me, God stopped His miraculous flow. There I was, looking over into Canaan. The word of the Lord was, "Get to work!" Suddenly, I had to dig my own wells. I found myself scheduling my spiritual, school and work life into seventeen-hour days. But as I entered the land and continued to obey God's Word as a faithful servant, He increased my responsibilities as we slowly possessed the land.

Possessing the land makes great demands of us. But the job is only getting done in certain small quarters because the expensive price of freedom remains unpaid in many lives. If most oppressed people had really understood the price of freedom before they cried out for it, they might have kept their mouths shut in favor of staying in Egypt. Why? It's more comfortable in Egypt for the slavery-minded oppressed. When you get over into the wilderness, there are tests and perils unheard of before. Then when you get into Canaan, you have to set your own schedule and get to work.

Let's take a look at some freedom misconceptions, and then move on to get the job done.

FREEDOM MISCONCEPTIONS

IN THIS CRUCIAL section I'm going to challenge your historical perception of freedom, and I am going to do it deliberately. Why? I want to damage your erroneous concepts of freedom so irreparably that you will walk away from this book with a new understanding of why the smells and slavery mind-set of Egypt have kept many bound in Sinai. I want you to get off the road to nowhere; I want you to get on the path to home. As you examine yourself through this knowledge, it is my hope that you will ask the Holy Spirit's help in turning your life around. It's time to put on your management hats, dig up your hidden talents, put them in the market and head into Jericho. No more circles in the desert! No more desert sand!

1. Freedom is the absence of laws and restrictions.

First of all, some people call freedom the absence of laws and restrictions. They don't want any laws; they just want to be free. "Don't tell me what to do!" they complain. "Don't put any limits or restrictions on me."

A sixteen-year-old comes to his parents and says, "That's it. You aren't going to run my life any more. I'm old enough now. I'm moving out of here. I'm tired of you telling me what to do. I'm going to pack my clothes. I'm gone. I want my freedom!"

A tear runs down his mother's cheek while this young fool is rambling on. He thinks she is crying because she doesn't want him to leave—and that's why he is a fool. But she isn't crying because of that. As a matter of fact, she would be glad to get rid of him if that's what he really wanted. What she is tearing up about is the fact that she said the same thing to her mother. This is why she knows that at sixteen he doesn't know how to run an apartment by himself. At his tender young age he doesn't know what it's like to bring up children or pay the utility bills. She would like to spare him all this trauma. But his concept of freedom is displacing his irresponsible lifestyle into a private apartment where he can "sleep" and watch TV all day. To him, freedom is the absence of laws and restrictions. And his misconception has him deceived. When he quits his first two jobs, he will come running home to Mama with a working understanding of freedom's responsibilities.

Some forty-five-year-old adults can sound like children with their complaints: "Hey!...I come to church when I can. So don't bother me. When I'm there, you should feel privileged that I came. There are many things on my schedule. So don't lay your rules on me. Just let me be free."

Is this you? Have you been deceived into believing that freedom is the absence of laws and restrictions? Freedom without law is anarchy. There is no freedom without law.

2. Freedom is void of work and obligation.

Like our fictitious sixteen-year-old in the previous misconception, many people think freedom means the absence of work. So they look to others in their "freedom" to take care of them. This misconception inevitably costs others the price of their laziness. It happens in the nation and in church. Like the hitchhiker I picked up that I mentioned in an earlier chapter, there are beggars wandering the wilderness of the church.

Jesus didn't die to birth moochers and beggars! But they certainly had them in the first-century church, and so do we. The man who planted that first-century church wrote, "If a man will not work, he shall not eat" (2 Thess. 3:10). You can't get more direct than that. If you want to experience God's lifestyle of freedom, your palms are going to have to come down out of the air to wrap around a shovel handle, because freedom takes hard work. Freedom demands more work than oppression.

3. Freedom is retirement from responsibility.

When the children of Israel were finally free from Pharaoh, suddenly they had no one telling them what to do. No more whips, bricks or pylon raisings. No more "Come here! Put your backs to it there! Time to eat!" or "Go to bed!" They were thankful to God for setting them free. But when Pharaoh wasn't there to direct them every day, their slavery mind-sets still needed him. They lacked the personal discipline to work independently. So they complained.

This is why so many in the world have such a discipline problem—they are living with Egyptian mind-sets in the wilderness of deliverance.

Why do you think we have to come up with game-show-like gimmicks to make people attend a church meeting? Why do you think we have to give out free food and all kinds of prizes to lure folks out to different church functions? It's because Pharaoh isn't there to force them to get up and out any more, and they still need a push. When fun and food are the reasons to get people in church, our gimmicks and games are "Pharaoh" for them.

I know I'm starting to tread on some toes now. But at

211

least the people who come out to win the barbecue grill do hear God's Word. And if you hear and receive enough Word, it can change a mind. Responsibility is in every jot and tittle recorded in God's holy Book. So I am glad that some people are open to our gimmicky appeals. It is our responsibility to make you responsible.

But once the games are over, it's time to go to the next level. It's time to start trading with the talent God has given. Responsible people will eventually own, not rent. They will trade with the talents God gave them and invest in a home or a church. Why give all your money to the money lenders? This will work for a while, but God wants everyone to manage their affairs well enough to possess their own property.

Now that we own our own building, we have the responsibility to maintain it. We can't call the landlord when we have a problem.

The first Sunday we were in our new facility, some of our church kids threw a whole roll of tissue paper in the toilet, and it stopped working. In fact, three or four of our toilets got clogged up because *our* children took *our* toilet paper and put it in *our* toilets that we bought, causing *our* toilets to stop up.

I went in the bathroom myself on Monday morning with the plunger. So here I was, the president of the company, down on my hands and knees working with a plunger. And you know what? It felt good, because this was my bathroom now.

If you want freedom, don't be thinking about retiring from responsibility. In fact, it will increase when your resources increase. So you better be ready to handle it. Freedom is hard work.

4. Freedom is relaxation.

Many people have this crazy dream: "By the time I turn forty years old, I want to be a millionaire." But when they imagine this, they're really dreaming about being free or retired from work and obligation with nothing to do but play golf all day, go shopping, watch TV or anything else they want to do. They don't understand that the kind of person who could earn millions of dollars wouldn't know what to do with twenty-four hours of leisure time a day. Millionaires have to wheel and deal and make things happen. That's how they made their million, and that's how they live. But many think, *When I make my million, I'll buy a seaside house and sleep or play golf.*

This misconception of freedom has probably done more damage to many than any other, because it has indoctrinated people with an escape mentality. Multitudes think that when they get to heaven they will be swinging on a hammock and drinking mint juleps in the backyard of their mansions, just whiling eternity away. They look at redemption like retirement, and it sadly affects the way they live on the earth.

Ultimate peace is in the "sweet bye and bye" according to so much of our prevalent religious thought. Nobody believes in this relaxation misconception more than Christians. We think of freedom as eternal relaxation. Our theology has promoted the idea of leaving the earth "finally" to enter the promised land for an eternity. In the meantime we spend our lives hiding out from the "evil, cruel world," without much thought for the welfare of the needs of the world.

May God deliver us from this spirit of deception. It's foolish to desire a life of nothing.

Freedom is not a vacation from earthly responsibilities and eternal realities; it is actually quite the opposite. *In freedom, we finally get to do everything ourselves. We get to see a need and meet it because it's the right thing to do.*

This erroneous escape theology has conditioned the church over the centuries to be irresponsible on the planet. Consequently, when the city becomes crime ridden, the youth go to drugs and the families fall apart, we say, "I'll fly away, oh, glory. Come quickly, Lord Jesus; take me out of this mess."

This is an ungodly attitude because it demonstrates that we don't care about the fallen, dying children of earth who are killing each other. Jesus died for these children, and He gave you the freedom to do something about it. We are to roll up our sleeves and use God's gifts to save the world from its bondage to sin. Paul writes:

> All this is from God, who reconciled us to himself through Christ and gave us the ministry of reconciliation.
>
> —2 CORINTHIANS 5:18

Instead, we pray for eternal relaxation, and sing. "When we all-l-l-l get to he-e-a-ven, what a day of re-e-joi-ic-ing that will be! When we all-l-l-l see-ee Je-sus, we'll sing and shout the vic-tory."[1]

We sing another song that goes like this: "When we cross over Jordan, we are going to sit down and rest a little

---

1. "When We All Get to Heaven" by Eliza Hewitt. Public domain.

while." And in our minds, a "little" is a billion, trillion years. We want to sit down next to that crystal lake, throw a bobber into the waters and take an eternal nap. Or we want to picnic by the pearly gates under the tree of anointing, pick golden apples and eternally strum on some harp. We just want to lie by the lake of righteousness for a million years doing NOTHING! And this idea of eternal relaxation produces irresponsible Christians who automatically want to go to heaven when they encounter problems.

The average Christian prays, "O God, how long, how long? Take me out of here, Lord. The world is so corrupt—murders and fights, killing and rapes. Come and take Your church out, Lord. Come, Lord. Rapture us now!"

But this isn't how Jesus thought. Look at the prayer He prayed the night before He died on the cross: "My prayer is not that you take them out of the world but that you protect them from the evil one" (John 17:15).

Now whose prayer is going to be answered, yours or Jesus'? Whose idea of freedom is God going to honor, yours or His? God isn't going to "move" us anywhere when times get tough, except forward into the battle. You may run and hide, but His direction is always forward—forward to the test—forward toward Jericho. So we aren't going anywhere to kick off our shoes, flop down on some celestial couch and pull the paper over our head. We have a responsibility—and it has nothing to do with eternal relaxation. *True freedom is permission to work and fulfill your potential.*

Now, as long as we're destroying misconceptions, I want to challenge your concept of heaven. In the apocalyptic writings of John, the apostle writes in his Book of Revelation these important words:

> Then I saw a new heaven and a new earth, for the first heaven and the first earth had passed away, and there was no longer any sea. I saw the Holy City, the new Jerusalem, coming down out of heaven from God, prepared as a bride beautifully dressed for her husband. And I heard a loud voice from the throne saying, "Now the dwelling of God is with men, and he will live with them. They will be his people, and God himself will be with them and be their God."
>
> —REVELATION 21:1–3

If you thought you were going to recline and eat grapes for the rest of eternity in heaven, John has news for you. According to God, you are coming back to earth to live in a holy city, and you aren't coming back to play and fly around. The new Jerusalem John saw descends *after* the thousand-year reign of Christ on earth as we now know it (with the curse removed). During that time Jesus will reign physically with His saints from Jerusalem—on earth.

> And they sang a new song: "You are worthy to take the scroll and to open its seals, because you were slain, and with your blood you purchased men for God from every tribe and language and people and nation. You have made them to be a kingdom and priests to serve our God, and they will reign on the earth."
>
> —REVELATION 5:9–10

Our work won't stop during the Millennium. We see this in Jesus' management parable of the minas taught in Luke 19, which parallels Matthew's teaching on the talents that we have looked at in depth.

> A man of noble birth went to a distant country to have himself appointed king and then to return. So he called ten of his servants and gave them ten minas. "Put this money to work," he said, "until I come back." ... The first one came and said, "Sir, your mina has earned ten more." "Well done, my good servant!" his master replied. "Because you have been trustworthy in a very small matter, take charge of ten cities."
>
> —Luke 19:12–13, 16–17

The distant country in this parable is the Bible's promised heaven where Jesus sits at the right hand of God right now, waiting for His enemies to be made a footstool for His feet (Ps. 110:1; Heb. 1:13). And the trading time is now for the people who will accept His minas and trade. Those who manage well will manage the resources and redemptive realities of earth's millennial cities. Wow! I didn't say it. Jesus did.

So forget those thoughts about eternal vacation when we enter eternity. Nowhere in the Bible does it say you are going to have huge plantation mansions, hammocks or wings. It may be in your hymn book—but it's not in the Bible. If you want to know what Scripture says about "life after death," read Revelation 5:10 and tell me if you see *work* in your future: "You have made them to be a kingdom and priests to serve our God, and they will reign on the earth." The word *reign* in this verse doesn't mean "to rest." It means to "exercise kingly power; to administrate, to execute judgment, to rule, to dominate a territory." It's hard work. God created every tongue and nation to reign with Him and dominate the earth. So you better get used to it in the here and now, because you are going to do it forever. Your destiny is responsibility—your future is freedom to work, to dominate and to rule.

5. Freedom is the release from external control.

This fifth freedom misconception speaks to the kind of rebellious thinking every person has had to deal with since Adam's fall. Since all people believe they are free when no one is controlling them, they desire to be even freer from external control. This means they want to be left alone by employers, pastors, presidents—whomever.

I need to emphasize the word *external* when talking about this kind of control. God actually intended for Adam to be free in his own freedom from external control. But Adam mismanaged his freedom. He was not mature enough to handle it—and neither are we.

To many, freedom is the freedom to be "left alone" so they can do what they want to do when they want to do it without anyone to answer to. This is not freedom; this is anarchy.

It is a sign of babyhood when someone must exercise external control by checking the one they are supervising to see how that person is doing. It's like caring for an infant. You have to check a baby every hour to see if he rolled over and suffocated. You check to see if he's burping or whether there is stuff in his mouth. That's external control.

218

Many Christians flirt with sin to see how close they can get to the fire without getting burned. They may have been converts for ten years, but they're still children. They think no one is watching their actions, and they read you the riot act if you challenge their lifestyles. They think they are free to sin because, after all, God will forgive them—so too bad for you if their sin affects you! But remember the fifth mismanagement principle from chapter four: Mismanagement may be "personal," but it is never "private." When this group sneaks around in its "freedom" from control, everyone around it can be affected. Achan thought no one would know about his pilfered silver. Ananias and Sapphira thought they had fooled everyone.

Among the many other responsibilities God is calling us to shoulder in our day, loving confrontation is on the top of the list. As a pastor, counselor and advisor, I know how rough growing up can be when people are suddenly challenged to take the wheels of their lives and drive straight—even when no one is looking. But this is where God's Word and the Holy Spirit help us in growth. A mature person knows that God is always watching—he doesn't need a chaperon to watch him anymore. I pray the day will come when we can live on *convictions* instead of *corrections*. A day when God will bring us to the point where *principles* instead of *punishment* guide us. But until then, God has placed mentors and other "external controls" in our lives to help us produce and grow.

Freedom is not the absence of external control as some think. Neither is it the absence of laws or work. It is not retirement or continual vacation time. Freedom is the responsible adherence to the laws and principles of God in the process of fulfilling your purpose for His glory.

> **A sense of responsibility is the clearest indication of maturity.**
>
> —JOHN MAXWELL

PRINCIPLES OF FREEDOM

CHAPTER 9
RESPONDING TO FREEDOM'S CALL

1. Freedom misconceptions:
   a. Freedom is the absence of laws and restrictions.
   b. Freedom is void of work and obligation.
   c. Freedom is retirement from responsibility.
   d. Freedom is relaxation.
   e. Freedom is the release from external control.
2. In freedom, we finally get to do everything ourselves. We get to see a need and meet it because it's the right thing to do.
3. True freedom is permission to work and fulfill your potential.

TEN

RESPONDING TO
RESPONSIBILITY

A word to Third World nations—
There is no greater burden than freedom,
no heavier load than liberty.

THE DESIRE AND passion for freedom is inherent in the human spirit. Every member of the human family carries the silent cry of freedom in the secret chambers of the heart. Regardless of the ethnic, cultural, social or political context of the individual, the need to feel valued, important and significant is paramount in the human experience. This truth is evident in the almost natural phenomena of civil struggles and uprisings in former colonial territories throughout the world in the past century.

The era of imperial expansion was the result of the age of discovery, which motivated small European nations to expand their political, economic and military status through world exploration expeditions. This aggressive need for imperial supremacy resulted in the invasion, subjugation, mutilation—and, in some cases, annihilation, oppression and enslavement—of millions of people throughout the world. This era, known as the *colonial era*, was a period when many of these cultures and peoples were dispossessed, relocated, traded and placed under the domination of imperial powers.

Colonialism is the imposition and colonizing of territories by an imperial power, usually through force and subversion. Most of this inhumane activity took place under the sophisticated, political systems and monarchies of Europe. The principal nations leading this period of history were Great Britain, Portugal, France and Spain.

The process of colonialism involved the capturing of territories and the claim of sovereignty and the imposition of authority over these captured territories. It brought the subjugation of natives, the establishment of foreign domination and the control of all resources and development. In many cases the resources were taken from the territories and exported back to the mother country or imperial power. In order to maintain control of these territories, the need for wealth, resources and manpower to defend and secure them became a primary objective of these imperial powers.

Consequently, the development of economically viable trade activity in nearly all these territories was inevitable. This context became the foundation of the slave trade. Trading in human slaves is not new. It can be traced back to the biblical days of the Pharaohs. It continued to show its inhumane head throughout the civilizations of the Babylonians, Greeks, Romans and Europeans. Western expansion of European imperialism introduced slavery to our hemisphere and exported the spirit of slavery throughout the world.

Trading in human slaves became the most lucrative form of economic wealth for millions—and the damnation of the lives of even more multiplied millions.

The nature of the slave trade, on the one hand, was the displacement of people to areas and territories to work as human chattel for the benefit of imperial aspiration and greed. In other territories, imperial powers moved in and took over the territories, subjecting the native population to forced labor and slavery. In both cases, the result was the disenfranchisement of human potential and the suppression, oppression and dehumanizing of millions of people.

These individuals were stripped of their dignity, self-worth, self-esteem, self-respect and sense of value. In extreme cases, they were even stripped of their humanity. Calculated, premeditated systems of control, desensitization and total emasculation caused emotional and mental damage that still exists today.

The products of these imperialist programs are identified today as Third World developing and undeveloped countries. It is just during the last seven decades that these former colonial territories, after many years of struggle, have obtained the opportunity to pursue their own destiny as a people and nations. Why are they called Third World? And what are the characteristics of a Third World nation?

THE EMERGING THIRD WORLD

THE CONCEPT OF Third World was introduced during a meeting of the G-5 nations (France, Germany, Japan, the United Kingdom and the United States) many years ago when they met to discuss the future development of the global economy. It is said that it was a French economist at that time who, in an attempt to describe the different categories of economic situations, suggested that there were three worlds on the planet.

The first world is known as the old world of Europe, which had been built on the agricultural society and governed by the systems of feudal lords and local kings. The second world is known as the New World, which described the discovery and settlement throughout the Americas, both North and South. This era was also known as the Industrial Revolution, which laid the foundation for our modern mechanical and technical societies. The final world, known as the Third World, describes the billions of people in territories that became the victims of oppression through subjugation and slavery.

The general definition of Third World nations refers to people who were not allowed to participate or benefit from the Industrial Revolution, despite the fact that the sweat and blood of these people became the human slab on which the foundation of the Industrial Revolution was laid.

This oppression is seen throughout every territory where colonialism or slavery was allowed to flourish. Today there are over six billion people on Planet Earth, and over four billion of them live in nations categorized as Third World. Many of these newly formed countries have been raped of their natural resources and wealth and are left without the tools, skills and machinery necessary to compete in this highly industrialized and technically driven world of the twenty-first century. Note that the definition of Third World covers the majority of the human population—a significant fact because it means these nations are now the object of God's attention. Therefore, they must understand their purpose in this new era.

These nations are the last worlds to experience the true freedom the Creator intended for all men. However, the process of achieving this quality of freedom has been, for most of these nations, an exercise in frustration, disillusionment and confusion at best.

A brief review of the young history of these embryonic nations and developing countries will reveal the drama of political instability, economic disaster, social turmoil, cultural confusion and spiritual conflict. Many Third World nations and people seem to suffer from the same symptoms—identity crisis, work ethic deficiency and lack of purpose, vision and self-confidence.

The continent of Africa testifies of the struggle of Third World developing nations to find their place in the global scheme of economic opportunity, political progress, social advancement and cultural identity. The Caribbean nations are no different, as many of these colorful nations emerging from the smoke of the fires of slavery consist of the products of Africa, Asia and the Far East. South American nations like Brazil, Chile, Argentina, Colombia, Peru and Venezuela, and the nations of the former Soviet bloc, are also suffering from the same scars of oppression. The question is, Why has the struggle for freedom and progress in all of these formerly oppressed colonized nations ended in the present cloud of despair? Why did it seem so easy for these nations to obtain deliverance from imperial colonial oppression and to achieve political independence, but not to experience the freedom they anticipated? The answer lies in the very nature of freedom and oppression.

This answer is the same for the individual and for the nation. The principles that guarantee true freedom were established by God the Creator. They can be observed through the prototype of the formation of the nation of Israel from a band of slaves in Egypt to a nation of significance, wealth, prosperity, stability, culture and moral strength. The laws and precepts by which this national miracle was accomplished are available to all nations, communities and individuals to follow if they desire to experience true freedom. Let us take a look at this model for national freedom and apply its principles to our lives and nation.

THE PRINCIPLE AND POWER OF OPPRESSION

IN THE BIBLICAL record of the memoirs of the great deliverer Moses, the story of oppression begins with the death of Joseph, prince of Egypt, at the age of one hundred ten. Joseph, a Hebrew by birth, was adopted by the daughter of the Pharaoh of Egypt and was regarded as a son of the king. The second book of the Bible, which Moses wrote, details the exodus of the Israelites from Egypt. The drama opens with the rising of a new king who did not know the generation of Joseph. He reduced the entire population of Hebrews to slaves, placing slave masters over them.

> Then a new king, who did not know about Joseph, came to power in Egypt. "Look," he said to his people, "the Israelites have become much too

numerous for us. Come, we must deal shrewdly with them or they will become even more numerous and, if war breaks out, will join our enemies, fight against us and leave the country." So they put slave masters over them to oppress them with forced labor, and they built Pithom and Rameses as store cities for Pharaoh.... They made their lives bitter with hard labor in brick and mortar and with all kinds of work in the fields; in all their hard labor the Egyptians used them ruthlessly.

—EXODUS 1:8–11, 14

These statements remind us that oppression is not a new phenomenon. It has been a practice of human rulership since the disobedience of man in the Genesis account. The Israelites remained in Egypt for over four hundred years, most of which were under the debilitating scourge of oppressive slavery.

Oppression can be defined as the imposition of external domination on another person to the point of controlling their physical, mental and spiritual aspirations. *Oppression is the cancellation of self-determination and the suffocation of personal potential.* The human spirit was created to dominate. This purpose was established by God in the creation of mankind.

Let us make man in our own image, in our likeness, and let them rule over the fish of the sea and the birds of the air, over the livestock, over all the earth.

—GENESIS 1:26

Any attempt to dominate, control, suppress, restrict and oppress the human spirit will ultimately fail. The natural desire to be liberated will always win over oppression because of this natural spirit of dominion.

As is the case in every situation of oppression, the cry for freedom rose up like smoke from the fiery pain of the broken Israelite spirit. The Creator, God, the Lord of heaven and earth, heard their cry and answered:

> I have indeed seen the misery of my people in Egypt. I have heard them crying out because of their slave drivers, and I am concerned about their suffering. So I have come down to rescue them from the hand of the Egyptians and to bring them up out of that land into a good and spacious land, a land flowing with milk and honey.... So now, go. I am sending you to Pharaoh to bring my people the Israelites out of Egypt.
>
> —EXODUS 3:7–8, 10

As we study the adventure and process of this great act of deliverance, there is a pattern that reveals definite principles established by God in the process of freedom that are consistent throughout the biblical text for personal, community and national liberation. Let us now look at these principles and apply them to our lives and national context.

UNDERSTANDING THE NATURE OF OPPRESSION

THE GOAL OF oppression is to achieve complete control and domination over the human spirit. Oppression attempts to destroy the desire for self-determination. This is done by a process of mental conditioning known as "breaking the spirit." This is called the possessing of the soul. The soul consists of the mind, the will and the emotions. This process usually begins with the restriction of physical freedom, movement and exposure to the environment. The objective is to control the physical environment so as to influence the mental, emotional and spiritual state of the individual. This process also includes control of access to resources and information. This is why historically, in every case of national communal oppression, the oppressor's grip on access to education and travel became imperative. The principle is that echoed by King Solomon, who stated in his proverb, "As he thinketh in his heart, so is he" (Prov. 23:7, KJV). Please note the use of the word *heart,* which refers to the subconscious mind or the seat of reasoning. *To control a man, a community or a nation, one must control the information content that enters the subconscious mind.* In essence, the ultimate goal and objective of oppression is to dictate and control the subconscious mind.

This principle is the source of spiritual oppression. In the biblical record of the first temptation in Genesis 3, the tempter first planted the idea of not being like God in the "heart"—or mind—of Eve. Then he introduced the thought of becoming like God through disobedience. This is always the method of destruction of the human spirit. It is the reason why Paul, the great apostle of the early church, declared, "We demolish arguments and every pretension that sets itself up against the knowledge of God, and we take captive every thought to make it obedient to Christ" (2 Cor. 10:5).

Jesus Christ, in His discourse with His disciples, further stated: "Those things which proceed out of the mouth come forth from the heart; and they defile the man" (Matt. 15:18, KJV). He continued, "For out of the heart proceed…the things which defile a man" (vv. 19–20, KJV). The biblical imperative to "repent" underscores the place and power of the soul (mind, will and emotion). The word *repent* literally means "to change one's mind or way of thinking." *Nothing changes until the subconscious mind changes.* Therefore, oppression is effective and complete when the soul surrenders. This process is the breaking of the spirit of the mind.

One of the greatest impacts of imperialist and colonial oppression on the billions of people in developing Third World countries is the mental damage caused by the oppressive philosophies of the oppressor. Even though oppression begins as an external experience, the ultimate effect is the resulting mental and psychological bondage.

THE EFFECTS OF OPPRESSION

A CAREFUL STUDY of the effects of oppression will reveal that it has an impact both on the oppressed and on the oppressor. *Oppression begins with the destruction of an individual's self-worth and sense of self.* It dismantles one's concept of self and value, and creates a lowered estimation of one's humanness. *Oppression brings a dissolution of a sense of purpose and meaning to life, reinforced by a spirit of hopelessness and despair.* Self-doubt and depression become commonplace among the oppressed, resulting in an immobilizing form of self-hatred, an inferiority complex, fear and the veneration of the oppressor.

The effects are further compounded by the environment of forced labor, which creates negative attitudes toward work, personal initiative, self-motivation and a sense of personal pride and accomplishment in work. The atmosphere surrounding oppressor-controlled lifestyles, schedules and activities destroys the spirit of creativity, constructive thinking, long-range planning and hope for a future for oneself or family.

The toll on the social structure of the family is perhaps the greatest negative impact on the oppressed. In many cases, individuals are separated from their original family community, which destroys the sense of heritage, history, belonging and significance to a human community. Many formerly oppressed people are still suffering after many decades from the aftereffects of this component of an oppressive system. In many communities, the family structure has been destroyed, and the very concept of an ideal family is nonexistent. In the Caribbean, Africa and South America, this is the source of many social problems today.

The conditions of the oppressed children in Egypt, the separation of Moses from his parents and his subsequent adoption by the daughter of Pharaoh all give evidence of the impact oppression can have on the nuclear family structure. The psychological disorientation resulting from the disruption of the family unit through enslavement and oppression reduces the social and cultural fabric necessary for healthy assimilation into the larger community.

Oppression also forces the disruption of the patriarchal role of providing for the family. This causes a sense of inadequacy, shame and a dysfunctional leadership role among the males within the framework of the family unit. In many cases, the traditional role of the male factor to provide and protect his family is destroyed, producing a spirit of failure, depression, frustration and despair. This leads to suppressed anger and bitterness, which manifests itself in many violent ways, including harmful antisocial behavior, dysfunctional family relationships and domestic abuse.

Oppression produces a deep spirit of dependency and lack of self-confidence. Oppression can become a habit, a lifestyle and a way of living. In fact, oppression can become a norm among the oppressed, so much so that any attempt to thwart the condition of oppression may be seen as a threat to security. This is a paradox, but history has ample evidence of this cruel reality.

In the case of the children of Israel, when Moses went to speak to them of the possibility of deliverance, it took a long period of convincing just to get them to concur.

> When they left Pharaoh, they found Moses and
> Aaron waiting to meet them, and they said, "May
> the LORD look upon you and judge you! You have
> made us a stench to Pharaoh and his officials and
> have put a sword in their hands to kill us."
> —EXODUS 5:20–21

Moses complained to the Lord about their complaints, saying:

> If the Israelites will not listen to me, why would
> Pharaoh listen to me, since I speak with faltering
> lips?
> —EXODUS 6:12

Oppression can become such a stronghold in the mind and life of the oppressed that they have to be persuaded toward the prospect of freedom.

There are no stronger words expressed to show the tremendous grip that oppression can have on the human spirit than those spoken by the Israelites even after they were delivered from Egypt.

> They were terrified and cried out to the LORD. They said to Moses, "Was it because there were no graves in Egypt that you brought us to the desert to die? What have you done to us by bringing us out of Egypt? Didn't we say to you in Egypt, 'Leave us alone; let us serve the Egyptians'? It would have been better for us to serve the Egyptians than to die in the desert!"
> —EXODUS 14:10–12

It is ironic that after years of crying out for freedom, when the opportunity for freedom did arrive, they desired slavery and oppression over the prospect of freedom.

The final effect of oppression on the oppressed is the spirit of immediate gratification at all cost. The oppressed see material things as a symbol of power, freedom and equality. This comes from having your life controlled and dictated to by the oppressor. It happens when restrictions and limitations are put on the obtaining of material things. It is the result of the prospect of having no future other than that designed by the oppressor. In essence, the standards and lifestyle of the oppressor become the measure of freedom and personal value of the oppressed. As a result, the oppressed begin to see the obtaining of the same status symbols of the oppressor as the ultimate pursuit in their desire to achieve personal freedom.

The result of these effects is that whenever the oppressed are given an opportunity to pursue their desire to be free, the passion for material possessions preoccupies their lives. This pursuit for materialism becomes an overriding force, causing them to sacrifice long-term permanent progressive planning for immediate temporary satisfaction with fading symbols. In many developing countries this is a major source of anti-social behavior and crime. Individuals pursue the symbols of status—at the expense of protection and respect for one another. This is a sign of oppressed minds.

THE EFFECT OF OPPRESSION ON THE OPPRESSOR

MANY WHO HAVE been victims of oppression harbor deep bitterness, hatred, suspicion and antagonism against the former oppressor and the symbols of oppression. But oppression does not affect only the oppressed. It is important to note that the oppressor is also oppressed—and the source of his oppression is the perceptions, attitudes and concepts he has developed toward the oppressed. Many oppressors have been affected by an insidious form of brainwashing, which has produced a mental disease that makes it nearly impossible for the oppressor to renew his mind with regard to the value, worth and equality of the formerly oppressed. This form of oppression—revealing itself as the sense of superiority—must be dealt with just as the oppressed need to be delivered from the spirit and mental conditioning of an inferiority complex.

After generations of an advantaged position, the oppressor also suffers from a false sense of security, and sees his lifestyle threatened by the prospect of equality with the formerly oppressed. In essence, the oppressor derives his sense of superiority from the maintenance of the inferiority of the oppressed. Equality of value, worth and estimation would cancel the gulf between the oppressor and the oppressed. I have had occasion to speak to many children of the oppressor. They express their frustration, confusion and anger over the fact that although they truly desire to accept and appreciate the equality of the oppressed, they find that doing so is almost an impossible task for them. Therefore, *both the oppressed and the oppressor need deliverance before true freedom can be embraced and experienced by both.*

In all of the formerly oppressed nations of the Third World and developing countries, the above effects of oppression can be found in different degrees—some on a conscious level and others on a subconscious level. The spirit of timidity, fear, distrust and immediate gratification prevail.

UNDERSTANDING THE PROCESS TO FREEDOM

IN THIRD WORLD nations, the march to freedom has been a long one, and many are still frustrated and disappointed about the illusive nature of true freedom. A brief study of the process established by God for the freedom of the children of Israel will reveal the fact that freedom is not as simple as first thought. Let us take a brief look at the principles of the biblical model for freedom.

1. God always promises you freedom while you are enslaved and oppressed.

2. God always raises up a deliverer to bring the people out of physical oppression. The *deliverer* must never be confused with a *freedom fighter*. In most cases, the deliverer is never the same as the freedom fighter (as in the examples of Moses and Joshua).

3. God never takes oppressed people directly to freedom: "So God led the people around by the desert road toward the Red Sea" (Exod. 13:18).

4. God always leads the people into a stage of deliverance. This is called the Sinai stage, or the desert phase.

5. God always provides miraculously in the deliverance phase. This is always a period of wealth and provisions: "The Lord had made the Egyptians favorably disposed toward the people, and they gave them what they asked for; so they plundered the Egyptians" (Exod. 12:36).

6. The purpose for the deliverance phase is to provide for the mental training and attitude transformation of the oppressed. The desert is the classroom for the graduation to freedom.

7. God will never take a people to the land of freedom until He has taken the land and the lifestyle of Egypt from their minds. (All the people who left Egypt died in the wilderness except Joshua and Caleb.)

237

8. God is willing to wait for the right generation to go to the land of true freedom. (He
   took *the children* of the former slaves into
   the Promised Land.)

9. God always raises up a new leader to take
   the people to freedom.

10. When the people arrive in the land of true
    freedom, the miraculous stops, and work and
    responsibility begin. Freedom demands
    responsibility: "The day after the Passover,
    that very day, they ate some of the produce of
    the land: unleavened bread and roasted grain.
    The manna stopped after they ate this food
    from the land; there was no longer any manna
    for the Israelites, but that year they ate of the
    produce of Canaan" (Josh. 5:11–12).

11. In freedom you must grow your own food,
    sew your own clothes and plant your own
    food.

12. In freedom you must fight your own battles
    (as in the example of Jericho being taken by
    Joshua and the Israelites).

MODERN DAY PARABLES

IN LIGHT OF these principles, we can analyze the process
of this journey to freedom for many nations and com-
munities in our modern context. For example, Martin
Luther King, Jr. was a deliverer for the Blacks in
America, but true freedom is yet to be realized. Nelson
Mandela was a deliverer for the victims of apartheid,

but the leader who will take them to true freedom will be another. It is important to note that Mr. Mandela understood and was willing to step down after his role was completed. Gandhi was the deliverer for the Indians from the colonial oppression of Great Britain, yet he was not the one to lead them into true freedom. The list goes on for many developing nations in the Caribbean and on the continents of Africa, Asia and Europe.

Each one of these principles is necessary for individual personal freedom, community freedom and national freedom. All of these principles apply to the journey to spiritual freedom from sin through salvation to spiritual maturity.

What Is True Freedom?

THERE IS TRULY no greater burden than freedom, no heavier load than liberty. The security of slavery and oppression is the absence of responsibility. The comfort of oppression is the absence of self-determination. The attraction of subjugation is the privilege of blame. In essence, slavery and oppression are attractive to the oppressed—they make the oppressor responsible for the lives and conditions of the oppressed. More men are afraid of freedom than they are of slavery and oppression. For many, the cry of freedom ends in the murmur of regret.

So what do we mean when we say we want to be free? What is true freedom? For many, freedom has been perceived as the absence of laws and restrictions and work and obligation. It is thought to be retirement from responsibility, the right to do as one pleases and release from external controls. All of these concepts of freedom are erroneous, but they are dangerously embraced by a great segment of our nations. However, true freedom is more costly and demanding than any form of slavery or oppression.

True freedom imposes more laws…demands more work…and requires more responsibility than slavery. Freedom demands that you do the right thing; true freedom imposes the need for more control than slavery.

The word *freedom* is derived from the mandate given by God to Adam to dominate and manage the earth. In essence Adam was commanded to be free to dominate the planet for God's glory. Thus we derive the word *free-dominate,* or *freedom.* True freedom is the right and opportunity to dominate the earth through the inherent gift one received from the Creator. Freedom is not the domination of another human being, but of the earth. Freedom is essential to all moral responsibility, and moral responsibility is one of the institutions of the human mind. However, freedom demands and could be defined as responsibility. There is no freedom without responsibility. *Freedom is the delegated right and release of authority to be responsible for governing and managing your designated sphere of influence through your natural gift in the fulfillment of God's purpose for your life.*

True freedom, therefore, makes you responsible and accountable to God. Freedom is God's delegated right for every man to dominate and govern and rule the earth, thus freedom is always within the law of delegation. There is no freedom without law. Freedom is not the absence of work or the cancellation of responsibility, but rather is the release to work and the assignment of responsibility. Responsibility is the greatest mark of maturity, both spiritually and mentally. Deliverance is instantaneous, but freedom is a process. We must always remember that deliverance may not necessarily lead to freedom. Deliverance is not the same as freedom. *Deliverance is release* from the oppressor, but *freedom is deliverance* from oppression. In essence, it is possible to be delivered and not to be free.

Freedom cannot be legislated. It is the result of revelation knowledge of one's true self and value. Remember that the power of the oppressor is the maintenance of ignorance. Jesus Christ, when speaking of true freedom in John 8, said these words: "You will know the truth, and the truth will set you free...if the Son sets you free, you will be free indeed" (John 8:32, 36).

These words clearly imply that freedom is more a matter of knowledge and understanding than of physical release from bondage. The apostle Paul said that a man can only be transformed by having his mind renewed (Rom. 12:2). The delivered must be trained for freedom. Most Christians are delivered spirits with oppressed minds. Sudden freedom can overwhelm a slave and drive him back into slavery. Freedom must not be confused with independence. The great king Solomon wrote some words that are filled with wisdom for our nations and our personal lives in Ecclesiastes 10:5–18. A portion of his words says, "Woe to you, O land whose king was a servant" (v. 16).

The implication is that when a formerly oppressed person is suddenly given power and authority, the prospects for good leadership are dim. Many of our developing nations are suffering from this principle, which denotes that wearing a crown does not change your mind. A delivered body does not guarantee a free mind. The only road to true freedom is self-discovery in God the Creator, and the prescribed way to Father God is through His Son, Jesus Christ. Only the manufacturer knows the truth about the product, therefore, the only One who knows the truth about you is God Himself. Freedom is discovering and embracing your true self and becoming all you were born to be. After return to the Father, transformation through the Son is admonished, and you must surrender to the work of God's Holy Spirit. Through the written Word, He will begin the process of renewing your mind so that you can learn the truth about yourself and your fellow men.

Only the truth can truly make you free.

PRINCIPLES OF FREEDOM

CHAPTER 10
RESPONDING TO RESPONSIBILITY

1. Oppression is the cancellation of self-determination and the suffocation of personal potential.
2. The goal of oppression is to achieve complete control and domination over the human spirit.
3. To control a man, a community or a nation, one must control the information content that enters the subconscious mind.
4. Nothing changes until the subconscious mind changes.
5. Oppression begins with the destruction of an individual's self-worth and sense of self.
6. Oppression brings dissolution of a sense of purpose and meaning to life, reinforced by a spirit of hopelessness and despair.
7. Oppression produces a deep spirit of dependency and lack of self-confidence.
8. Both the oppressed and the oppressor need deliverance before true freedom can be embraced and experienced by both.
9. True freedom imposes more laws...demands more work...and requires more responsibility than slavery.
10. Freedom is the delegated right and release of authority to be responsible for governing and managing your designated sphere of influence through your natural gift in the fulfillment of God's purpose for your life.

ELEVEN

FREE AT LAST

In reading the lives of great men, I found that the
first victory they won was over themselves—
self-discipline with all of them came first.
—*HARRY S. TRUMAN*

FREE AT LAST ... free at last ... thank God Almighty, I'm
free at last!" These powerful words of America's great
civil rights deliverer, Martin Luther King, Jr., stunned the
world as he spoke them to millions over radio and TV in
the 1960s. Dr. King, like Nelson Mandela in South
Africa, Gandhi in India and other lesser-known social
deliverers around the world, laid down his life and
future to make civil rights available to the world's disadvantaged communities. But these men, as great as their
efforts proved, were only their followers' deliverers,
because freedom is a matter of the mind. Men can
deliver you, but it is what you know that makes you free.

Today millions of the followers whom these great
civil rights leaders gathered are still prisoners in their
minds. *True freedom is a matter of the mind—not of
human law.* And true freedom involves much more

work than does slavery—because freedom imposes more restraints on an individual than does slavery.

THE ESSENCE OF FREEDOM

FREEDOM IS THE discovery of truth about yourself. Truth brings freedom. True freedom will liberate you to become all you were created to be. It gives liberty to work within the laws of life. Under slavery you are under another's law. A whip is used to enforce that law. But when you come into freedom, you must obey internal laws. The pressure is on you to keep those laws by yourself. Freedom is self-imposed discipline.

If you were my slave on a nineteenth-century cotton plantation, I could post ten things on the wall of the slave house with which you would be required to comply daily. When you got up in the morning, you would know exactly what to do. You wouldn't even have to think or plan your day. Your every waking moment would be set out for you down to the minute—and I would do the planning.

If one day I chose to set you free, you would have your own house in your own community, but through the gaining of your freedom you would lose my ten rules. Suddenly you would be thrust into a world with thousands of alternatives, and you would have to choose which choices were best for you. You would have to live right without anyone watching you. Remember, discipline is remembering what you want.

That is the truth of living free. You must freely choose your own laws for living, and you must live with the con- sequences of your choices. *Freedom is taking responsi- bility for your life. It is designing your own destiny and deciding your own consequences.* Let's take a closer look at some principles of freedom.

1. In freedom, you are the boss whether you work for another or not.

In freedom there is no one to blame for your victories or mistakes except yourself. You may be three generations out of the slave house, but if you are still blaming your culture for your problems, you are a long way from being truly free. This is why the apostle James writes, "Speak and act as those who are going to be judged by the law that gives freedom" (James 2:12). The law that gives freedom, says James, is God's law to choose freely. James instructs us to know and live in God's truth, which can change our minds and improve our behavior. *Freedom is a matter of the mind.*

When a man understands his freedom in relation to God, he will honor the laws of the land that don't violate God's law. The laws of man were never intended to be permanent fixtures. Legal statutes have been fashioned as regulatory principles to allow people to remain in society and to be productive. "If you don't do this," the law of man says, "we will allow you to live freely outside of our jails to do whatever you want to do within the limits of the law."

In his first letter to Timothy, Paul writes:

> We know that the law is good if one uses it properly. We also know that law is made not for the righteous but for lawbreakers and rebels, the ungodly and sinful, the unholy and irreligious; for those who kill their fathers or mothers, for murderers, for adulterers and perverts, for slave

traders and liars and perjurers—and for whatever else is contrary to the sound doctrine that conforms to the glorious gospel of the blessed God, which he entrusted to me.

—1 Timothy 1:8–11

Paul tells us that laws will always be necessary for those who act irresponsibly. *The less responsible you are, the more laws you need.* The more responsible you become, the less laws are required, because laws are intended to push you away from their requirements into the productivity of personal freedom.

The laws of God were handed down ultimately to lead men to freedom. But do you think God loves laws like "Thou shall not steal," "Thou shall not bear false witness" and "Thou shall not commit adultery"? I believe He hates those laws. But He had to establish them once Adam trespassed and stole the illegal fruit off the illegal tree. Society is so corrupt today that it can't handle the freedom of having a tin of tuna on the shelf by itself. Someone will snatch it if it's left unguarded. Leave a radio untended by your picnic table at the beach, and someone will come along to relieve you of it. Why? Because people, as a rule, can't handle freedom. So God imposes law.

Young people today are lawless because they are irresponsible. This is why children need laws, not negotiation, discussion or compromise. They can't handle freedom. Yet in many parts of the world, society has licensed their lawlessness by giving them rights as juveniles to be free from the penalty of law or the discipline of their parents.

God knows Adam's descendants can't keep their

hands off the five thousand dollars on the counter. He knows we humans need our "No Trespassing" signs to keep us out of jail. And Christians aren't immune. You know that, don't you? If you don't think that born-again, Spirit-filled Christians break the Ten Command-ments on any given day, you really don't know what is happening in the Christian world daily.

The church has been gifted with the Holy Spirit and God's convicting Word, which can allow us to keep the Ten Commandments. Paul writes:

> For what the law was powerless to do in that it was weakened by the sinful nature, God did by sending his own Son in the likeness of sinful man to be a sin offering. And so he condemned sin in sinful man, in order that the righteous require-ments of the law might be fully met in us, who do not live according to the sinful nature but according to the Spirit.
>
> —ROMANS 8:3–4

But if we neglect God's comfort and counsel, we can disobey God's "No Trespassing" signs as quickly as the unconverted.

You would be surprised how many Christians might steal a stapler or take some copier paper home from work because "everyone is doing it." Like others, they think they are "free to do it," while they break the law. The divorce rate in the church today is as high as in the world. And, yes, some Christians drink and even take drugs in the process of flunking a wilderness test.

God wants all men to live free, above the law, bound by a higher set of principles. This is why Jesus came—to all men—to save all. True freedom requires law, because freedom without law is anarchy. True freedom operates out of internalized laws based on the principles of God. *In essence, then, self-control and self-discipline are both attributes of true freedom because discipline is self-imposed law. This is freedom.*

> It is for freedom that Christ has set us free. Stand firm, then, and do not let yourselves be burdened again by a yoke of slavery.
>
> —Galatians 5:1

The freedom our Deliverer, Jesus, came to bring has nothing to do with externally imposed law. Freedom says, "Stealing is not in my principle of living." If I see ten cents or ten thousand dollars, they are both the same to me because the same principle is present: I don't steal because I think it's wrong. True freedom has nothing to do with staying out of jail through complying with any set of laws. There are freer convicted criminals behind bars who have found Christ's freedom in their prison chapels than the guards who pass in and out of their cells as free citizens every day.

True freedom comes from moving into the responsibility of crossing over Jordan in personal accountability to God and His Word. Jesus has proclaimed it and opened our prison doors, but we must take the responsibility to walk outside and be free. The decision is made in our mind. The major, dramatic difference we see between freedom and slavery is the fact that freedom is much harder to engage because of *personal* choice and accountability.

2. Freedom demands more work than slavery.

A second remarkable difference between freedom and slavery is that freedom demands more work than slavery. This doesn't seem to make sense, does it? Pharaoh oppressed the Israelites. He forced them to work, rise early, work hard and go to bed late. They were whipped when they worked slowly, and they were kicked, punched and spat upon when they rebelled. It was cruel and tough work.

Yet when you stop to think about it, freedom demands more work than slavery. Why? You will never qualify for freedom if you don't become industrious. When you seek God's will in the wilderness, He will administer your talents and send you to trade with the inhabitants in the promised land. You must take the land, and that takes WORK. There are no more instant miracles in Canaan. On the other side of the Jordan you must learn how to fast and pray to become a part of the miracle. You must milk the cow and scoop out the beehive to enjoy Canaan's milk and honey. It is there that Christ will hand you the money purse and give you the skills to fill it. You must work hard and maybe even fail at a business before you succeed. Management. Management.

I will never forget the scripture that changed my life years ago. It is found in the Book of Proverbs:

> He who tills his land will have plenty of bread, but
> he who follows frivolity will have poverty enough!
> —PROVERBS 28:19, NKJV

When I first read that verse, it frightened me. But I soon discovered that if we as a people don't take possession of our own territory, someone else will come and work it for us. If we as the church don't take responsibility for our own deliverance and freedom, we will soon find ourselves drifting back into Egypt.

The church is living in a new era of responsibility today. God is cutting off the manna and telling us to roll up our sleeves. We had better learn to do some planting and digging, because He is shutting down the water and cutting off the free food. We had better learn how to sew, because from here on, our clothes will wear out.

The time for playing religious games is time spent in the wilderness. But the days are now short, and God needs Joshuas to fill and replenish the earth before the time on earth's clock ticks slowly away. There is no more time to play with the toys of Egypt. When God delivers us from the wilderness, He brings us into responsibility. We must get the education, wisdom and faith to work with God, or we will end up back in slavery while the teachable are taking the land.

Oh, if you are converted by God's Holy Spirit, you will make heaven—I'm not saying you will backslide and go to hell. When you die in the wilderness, the angels will bring your soul to paradise. What I am saying is that if you don't learn to shoulder the burden of freedom in this new era of responsibility, you will remain ignorant and bound by the oppressor while God's Joshuas take the land.

God is calling Joshuas from every community and nation to live free, management-minded, productive lives. Freedom involves more work than slavery because the work begins on the inside. In freedom there is no one to shout, "Get up, slave!" There is no one to beat you into submission when your mind doesn't want to comply. In freedom you have to get up by yourself. You can't bury your talent in the ground and expect the government to pay your way. You have to get out of the house, go to the job and stay there until lunch time. You have to come back from lunch in one hour and stay there until five (sometimes later). You can't leave, slack off or play hooky. When you have to work overtime, you may be compensated for it when you work for someone else. But there isn't any extra pay when you finally trade with your talents to the place where you are working for yourself. Freedom is hard work.

I'll never forget the first day I went to the university. I thought I was going to die. I was brought up in the Bahamas under the British system in which everything was laid out for you. But when I walked into class at the university that first day, the professor walked in and said, "Read chapters one through five. God bless you all, and do a paper in the morning." Then he quickly left.

I watched his back as he walked out the door and sat there terrified, thinking, *Hey! Where are you going? Where's my teacher?* I ran out to catch him in the hall with my big, thick history book in hand and said, "Excuse me, sir. You just gave an assignment. Aren't you going to teach us?"

"Where are you from?" he asked.

Well, I knew from the tone of his voice that I was going to get a rebuke. "I'm from the Bahamas," I replied.

"That's a nice place," he said, "but this is college, and in college you teach yourself."

Well, let me tell you, when he said that, my whole body went into spasms. So I held up that thick history book and asked, "You mean I have to study this huge book myself?"

"Yes," he said. "I'm just a resource person."

You're just a resource person? A resource person? I thought, feeling sorry for myself.

Well, I got over it and made it a responsibility to get organized quickly. I had to make my own schedule for running, studying and reading. I cut out TV and didn't go for pizza with the other students. Suddenly, I found myself having to make and follow my own plans, and it took more responsibility than I had ever been entrusted with. But it taught and trained me in the ways of freedom.

Our kids have it easy when my wife, Ruth, and I remind them, "Homework time!" But when you grow up and go to college, there isn't anyone to "remind" you. Freedom is rough. You have to work extra hard—harder than you ever did when you were enslaved in bondage, because now you have to be responsible from the inside out.

3. Freedom requires more responsibility than slavery.

The mistakes you made in the wilderness could destroy you in Canaan. The requirements of responsibility are at a much higher level in Canaan. After the younger generation was circumcised on the other side of Jordan, they proved their disciplined training by marching silently around the gates of Jericho. Could you imagine? Not one spoken question or gripe about the redundant marching they were doing. (Now that's disciplined training. Their parents had complained with every wilderness step they took.) Then, on the seventh time around, this younger generation shouted as God had commanded, and Jericho's walls came down.

God has said that Israel would be invincible—and

now they knew it! Their next military objective was the little town of Ai. But no one knew that within their ranks was one man who had disobeyed God's command recorded in Joshua 6:18.

> But as for you, only keep yourselves from the things under the ban, lest you covet them and take some of the things under the ban, so you would make the camp of Israel accursed and bring trouble on it.
>
> —NAS

Jericho was an amazing victory, so Israel sent out spies to determine the number of troops it would take to destroy Ai. When they moved in to attack, "they were routed by the men of Ai, who killed about thirty-six of them" (Josh. 7:4–5).

God told Israel in the wilderness that they would win every Promised Land war. He said that He would be with them and that they would conquer the land. But now, because of *one man* by the name of Achan, the entire nation would have to pay the price. One man broke the law. But the Bible says, "The *Israelites* acted unfaithfully in regard to the devoted things" (emphasis added). Achan is singled out in the next sentence, but the entire nation of Israel was charged with his offense: "Achan son of Carmi, the son of Zimri, the son of Zerah, of the tribe of Judah, took some of them. So the LORD's anger burned against Israel" (Josh. 7:1).

Well, Joshua was completely confused about the whole situation and fell on his face before God. "What's wrong?" he asked. So God told him that someone had broken His law of the Jericho ban. Then without informing him of who the law breaker was, God told Joshua to deal with it by bringing every person before him "clan by clan. . . . He who is caught with the devoted things shall be destroyed by fire, along with all that belongs to him. He has violated the covenant of the Lord and has done a disgraceful thing in Israel!" (Josh. 7:14–15). Achan was stoned and burned, but not before thirty-six innocent men had to pay for his offense.

Once Israel crossed over into Canaan, God didn't want the Israelites to think about doing what Achan had done again. So the Lord had the camp stone and burn everything Achan loved and owned.

> Then all Israel stoned him, and after they had stoned the rest, they burned them.
>
> —Joshua 7:25

This new century into which we are moving won't be like the baby days of our instant-miracle revivals. We won't be able to get away with the baby sins of the wilderness once we cross over the Jordan into God's promised land of maturity. God is putting a heavy responsibility on us, and that is why we must watch for each other.

This isn't just Old Testament stuff. I believe we are heading back to the powerful days the early church experienced in the Book of Acts. Acts 5 tells us about a married couple by the name of Ananias and Sapphira who were struck dead because of lying about an amount of money they put in the offering plate. Verse 11 tells us, "Great fear seized the whole church and all who heard about these events."

The amount of money wasn't the issue; it was Ananias and Sapphira's lying that earned them the sentence of death. Like Achan, the couple lost their lives to stop their sin from spreading and killing others in the church community.

One man by the name of Achan stole and hid what God had instructed Israel not to touch. And because of his individual action, the entire nation was held to account. In freedom, everything you do affects someone else. If you neglect what you are supposed to do in your ministry, in your commitment, in your promise to others or in your business, it's no longer a personal thing. You can't just say, "I'm not showing up tonight." In freedom, when you don't show up, someone gets hurt. *True freedom doesn't presume the right to act without regard to the effect personal decisions would have on another's freedom. True freedom protects the freedom of others and acts responsibly on behalf of others.*

If you know someone who is sinfully mismanaging his life today, go to him personally. Take responsibility. Say, "Listen, I've been concerned about you. You've been living badly, and I want you to stop because you are messing up your family, the community and the church." There is little room for mistake when you're in the trenches fighting. It is time to start holding one another accountable. It is time to be responsible.

4. Freedom imposes more of the need for control than slavery.

We think of slavery as a lifestyle dominated by someone who has control over us. Yet freedom gives us the need for even more control. There is a slavery from which you can deliver yourself—like the slavery the Israelites experienced when they were bound in Egypt.

But there is also a slavery that you impose on yourself by your own irresponsible decisions. So, because of the eternal implications our decisions can have on ourselves and others every day, this principle of freedom declares our need for internal control.

The great church planter and apostle Paul mentioned this in 1 Corinthians 6:12 when he wrote, "Everything is permissible for me—but I will not be mastered by anything." I believe God is going to demand an account of everything that we do from now on.

We must exercise a kind of control in freedom that we didn't need in slavery—self-control. There are too many opportunities today to be lazy and controlled by external things. There are too many television sets and video machines invading and enslaving our homes. There are too many cable networks and Hollywood movies. And there are too many recreation sites and beaches with fast cars to get us there.

It's easy to control slaves held in bondage, because you can impose the whip. You can impose the gun. You can impose the dogs. You can threaten someone by withholding their food or by taking away any number of privileges.

But freedom has even more controls than slavery, because in freedom you have to control yourself. You are the one who says when you will or won't watch TV. You are the one who says you will or won't read. No one can force you to do anything in freedom, except you. And that is harder work than having someone impose controls on you.

You are responsible for getting yourself up and off to work in freedom. Then it is up to you to stay on the job once you get there. You are the one who must make your own budget and choose not to spend money on hamburgers when you need to pay the house rent. That's a lot of self-control, isn't it?

You are the one in freedom who gets to pass up the extra helping of barbecued chicken, rice and beans, macaroni and cheese and guava duff pastries for dessert. Don't you wish God would control your diet? I do. I hate buffets because they really test my responsibility. When I go down that long line of food, there isn't anyone to stop me, and my stomach shouts, "Cheese-cake, chicken and rice!" And it is then that the reality of appetite freedom can really hit. Your stomach says, "Stop!" But your eyes say, "More!" Don't you wish God would tell you what to eat and make you stop when it was enough? "That's it, My son. Thou shalt eat no more." Wouldn't that be great? You would have the shape you had ten years ago. Under the oppressor, he controlled when, what and how much you ate. There was no need for self-control.

But this just doesn't happen. And this is why one of the fruits of the Spirit is self-control (Gal. 5:23). If you don't control yourself, someone else will. A fruit isn't automatically bestowed, it grows. Joshua's Promised Land instruction of meditating on God's Word and allowing the Holy Spirit to circumcise the memory of our slavery in the past is so important in freedom. (See Joshua 1:8.)

So you see, in freedom you need more control than you do in slavery, because in slavery they give you a quarter of a rib and that's it. And when you have a measly quarter rib, you don't have the need to impose control on yourself.

We are all to grow up as spiritual examples and mature leaders. The Scripture instructs leaders to be self-controlled. Writing to his companion and fellow leader, Titus, the apostle Paul said a leader "must be blameless—not overbearing, not quick-tempered, not given to drunkenness, not violent, not pursuing dishonest gain. Rather he must be hospitable, one who loves what is good, who is self-controlled, upright, holy and disciplined" (Titus 1:7–8). To Timothy, Paul wrote that leaders must "first be tested; and then if there is nothing against them, let them serve" (1 Tim. 3:10).

Self-control is an attribute in freedom that slavery knows little about. The "if it feels good do it" mentality of the modern world is going to have to be purged from the twenty-first-century citizen as we put our feet in the Jordan in the years to come. I know, we would just love to be "twanged" with a holy staff like Moses carried at salvation, and live our lives completely controlled from above. But it doesn't happen that way. Freedom happens when we allow God to lead us out of the wilderness into the fruitful work of Canaan—from dependency to responsibility.

I expect to see millions of mature believers who are not afraid of a good fight before I die. I'm talking about people who will take on the biggest challenges, quite aware of what it takes to win. I long to see a generation who will embrace the spirit of responsibility and industry. A generation who can handle failure and success effectively.

I've never met a boxer who is world champion who didn't lose some rounds. No one remembers the losses when he holds the winner's belt. But back in the fourth round, there he was, bloody and all beaten up, barely making it back to the corner. His manager said, "You can get him." The boxer protested, "Are you crazy? I'm not going back out there. You go out there and see how you like it! I can't see, and my arms are tired." So the manager massaged him and told him he could do it. Then he doused him with water, made sure the butterfly bandage on his eye was secure, rubbed his shoulders and told him to go back out there and get that opponent.

That's what God does when you come back in from the fight of the day feeling as if you aren't going to make it. As you stand faithfully in your disciplined self-control, the Holy Spirit soaks you in your corner with His holy bucket of the Word and the sponge, and says, "You're going back out there, and you are going to fight!" Then He rubs your shoulders and reminds you, "Greater is He who is in you than he who is in the world. You can do all things through Christ who strengthens you. Now get out there and fight—take that land!"

Our days of running and hiding are over. You have to fight to get stuff out of life on the other side of Jordan. Jesus' wilderness experience speaks volumes to us. Following His baptism of the Spirit in the Jordan, the wilderness provided His testing ground, and He came out victorious in the anointing of God's power. From that day forward He worked in His calling of ministry, sometimes twenty-four hours a day, to fulfill God's will. His land of Canaan was teeming with the work of Satan, who had bound mankind in death. But Jesus dispossessed him, just as you are called to do in Haiti, Africa, America or wherever you live. To experience your true freedom you must successfully face and overcome the "ites"—the Moalites, Tebusites, Canaanites and all obstacles in the way of what God promised you.

MANAGEMENT!

THOSE OF US with ears to hear today can hear the Jordan rushing over the hill. We are at the end of our generation. God is saying, "Your wilderness days are gone. So get ready. Say good-bye to the manna. The easy ways are shutting down. Your long walk to nowhere is coming to an end." Get ready for responsibility. Get ready for work. Accept the wonderful burden of freedom and live at maximum.

Jesus is issuing swords and purses to His people around the world. Yes, the "ites" are in the land, and they won't bow just because it's Sunday and we're dressed to the hilt. But God will fight with us as we march over the hill.

What resources has God entrusted to you? What will you do tomorrow to discover and improve the talents He has entrusted to you? Easy miracles are for babies. Collaborative miracles are for sons. So let us move on into the twenty-first century as promised land sons and daughters who are competent in God's affairs.

People are made of the sum total of the choices and decisions they make every day. Management, management, management! It's time to move in!

**Decide your destiny! Accept your freedom.
Take your position. Respond to responsibility.**

Principles of Freedom

Chapter 11
Free at Last

1. True freedom is a matter of the mind—not of human law.
2. Freedom is taking responsibility for your life. It is designing your destiny and deciding your own consequences.
3. The less responsible you are, the more laws you need.
4. Self-control and self-discipline are both attributes of true freedom because discipline is self-imposed law. This is freedom.
5. True freedom doesn't presume the right to act without regard to the effect personal decisions would have on another's freedom. True freedom protects the freedom of others and acts responsibly on behalf of others.
6. We must exercise a kind of control in freedom that we didn't need in slavery—self-control!

You can experience more of God's grace & love!

*I*f you would like free information on how you can know God more deeply and experience His grace, love and power more fully in your life, simply write or e-mail us. We'll be delighted to send you information that will be a blessing to you.

To check out other titles from **Creation House** that will impact your life, be sure to visit your local Christian bookstore, or call this toll-free number:

1-800-599-5750

For free information from Creation House:

CREATION HOUSE
600 Rinehart Rd.
Lake Mary, FL 32746
www.creationhouse.com

Experience the Peak of Leadership...

Send For Your Free Trial Issue Today!

I f you're serious about leading your church into the 21st century, then *Ministries Today* is for you. Our No. 1 priority is to equip and encourage those on the "front lines" of ministry—pastors, group leaders, Sunday school teachers, youth pastors. Anyone involved in church leadership.

Ministries Today brings you new, innovative ideas. Learn what's working at other churches. Find timely advice, inspiration, even humor. Keep abreast of legal issues affecting the church. Stay tuned to what the Holy Spirit is doing around the world.

If you like what you see, then pay the invoice of $21.00 (**saving over 41% off the cover price**) and receive 5 more issues (6 in all). Otherwise, write "cancel" on the invoice, return it, and owe nothing.

Call 1-800-829-2547 for
1 Free Issue Trial Subscription
(offer #A0ACHB)